Also by William Rose Benét

DAY OF DELIVERANCE

A BOOK OF POEMS

THE DUST WHICH IS GOD

A NOVEL IN VERSE

These are Borzoi Books, published in New York
by ALFRED A. KNOPF

THE STAIRWAY OF SURPRISE

THE

STAIRWAY

OF SURPRISE

"Pass in, pass in," the angels say,
"In to the upper doors,
Nor count compartments of the floors,
But mount to paradise
By the stairway of surprise."

EMERSON : *MERLIN*

William Rose Benét

ALFRED A. KNOPF : NEW YORK : : MCM:XL:VII

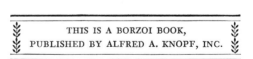

THIS IS A BORZOI BOOK,
PUBLISHED BY ALFRED A. KNOPF, INC.

FIRST EDITION

TO AMY LOVEMAN

We've seen a rampant quarter-century through
In work with hope. But what I've done to earn
The steady friendship of one so fine and true
Is nugatory as this small return.

CONTENTS

v

III. GALLERY

IV. THE FIRE IN THE CRYSTAL

I

CENTRE IS EVERYWHERE

"The nature of God is a circle of which the centre is everywhere and the circumference is nowhere."

EMPEDOCLES : *A LOST TREATISE*

SUPREME BEING

In the boulder on the shore, as though the core
Which is crystal in our granite were as glass
I saw the being that men believe no more,
The sleeping form Antæan. Thence to pass
Clambering from rocks to grey-walled pine and grass,
What breath was animate in the grass and flower
I knew, and where the grey-furred squirrel was
What fled through shadow and sun; and in that hour
It lived in me, confirming ancient writ;
Life of the stone, the life through nature flowing.
Then the changed light of day was full of it,
That superhuman truth too great for knowing.
Yet, while night loomed, the myriad stars in host
But watchfires seemed of His aërial coast.

HARMONY*

Master of music, wring again the strings,
wound the wide air with eddying chord on chord !
Something within me sings
and I would be delivered of a word,
word of creation,
word of wind and flame,
whereby am I its centre everywhere,
whence the hot clotted worlds from chaos came
to glitter like diamond on blue night air.

Melodic archer, bend the infinite bow
missiled with golden tones of rhythmic fire
like battle arrows with heads of blazing tow
arcing the dark rampire !
Twang the bow string, the harp string ! Of what whole
my part, none knows — music not mine in breath
or sinew — yet this harmony my soul summoneth. . . .

The harp frame racked from pedestal to crown,
vibrating life in pity and pain unending,
with great dim hands of shadow sweeping down,
some great vague visage bending. . . .

---

* "Materialists sometimes declare that the relation of conscious intelligence to the brain is like that of music to the harp, and when the harp is broken there is no more music. An opposite view, long familiar to us, is that the conscious soul is an emanation from the Divine Intelligence that shapes and sustains the world, and, during its temporary imprisonment in material forms, the brain is its instrument of expression. Thus the soul is not the music, but the harper. . . ."   *John Fiske*
    One theory of the invention of the harp is that its origin is in the warrior's or hunter's bow.

PELOPS

Food for the gods, brother of tears,
Son of the frustrate evermore,
Image of Man and all Man's years;
Inscrutable conspirator
Against the veiled Cumaean night;
Hammerer upon the iron door
Why-and-Wherefore;

We bare your shoulder and we see
What the voracious mother gave,
Devourer of what progeny,
Dragging whole empires to the grave.
Fixed in your flesh that pauldron white,
That badge of mercy which may save
In the stellar cave.

In the huge cavern of empty air
Where blow the gales that are most drear —
In the enormous Question where
Our only answer is our fear
Or tears that claim a greater myth —
Than your ensign the ivory sphere
Shines not more clear.

Thus by similitude we grope
And paraphrase and farse the song
Of stars and atoms with vain trope
To counter our devouring wrong
From Earth, and dream us Pelops' kith,
Our shoulders as his shoulder strong
Hope to prolong.

THE INCARNATE

God has the face of a beast, of a rock, of a flower.
He murmurs in foliage. In blind ocean his word is heard.
He is the visage of crowds, of clouds, and the eyes of your dear.
He is the stare of the tiger, the dry throat of fear.
His Janus face is the pitiable hour
When the slime of earlier aeons within you is stirred.
He glares in Lucifer as he shines in Jesus.
His ways are hardly to please us.
They are to exact, exalt, and ravenously to amend us.
God is our goad, our gadfly, our stinging vexation;
A spiritual temblor, an inner upheaval tremendous.
For God began and will end us.

The Lord is in his holy atom. . . .

Know you anything of awe, Babylonian generations?
When I would contemplate, my falseness moves
Through the abyss of self, or through Cytherean groves;
Yet by daylight I exult in the various creation.
God? In all the rooms of memory I find him
Where dreams at their looms still bind him and unbind him
As the shuttle moves. But only in good deeds
Spontaneous, impulsive with innocent love,
Is he immediate, neither remote nor above
Or a white anatomy on a cross that bleeds
Nor the bloody slayer in the forest, nor reptile lust.
No, then he is a whirlwind of gold upon our dust,
To every cankerous ill an anodyne,
To everlasting thirst through all our veins a roaring wine
Of intense creation; in the barren breast
The inconceivable conceiving moment of exquisite rest.

Let all our words and our wars keep silence before him!

6

I saw a man standing
    by a dark sea.
Strange was the word
    he said to me:
"A million scenes are in this scene;
through a million battles I have been."

I saw a man riding
    under a star.
Wild was the cry
    he cried from far.
I saw him come to a glimmering ford
and a myriad shadows beset his sword.

I saw a man questing
    under the moon,
through the unresting
    night of June.
In a myrtle bower I well knew of
he sobbed of the power and the pangs of love.

I saw a man reading
    under a dome
piled with high wisdom
    tome on tome.
The moth that around his candle flew
no more ephemeral was, I knew.

Under the eye
    of the open sky,

on a vast plain
   a man was I.
Before him a burning wheel did run.
He staggered after the rolling sun.

On inner space
   and outer space,
I saw the imprint
   of a face
awful and unparadised
yet with the living eyes of Christ;

the face of God
   with Man made one:
author of being
   and eidolon;
the opener of every door,
every symbol's secret core.

I saw a horseman
   beyond a stream
that roiled and boiled
   with the shapes of dream;
but ere his accost had brought me light,
he spurred and was lost in the wood of night.

DARK PLANET

Once at the edge of night ere day breaking
I heard a voice say hush to the toiling mind:
Soon will come an end to the long aching
    Of hoodman blind.

Earth no more will be steeped in dire murder,
Nation snarl at nation or life betray;
Light will glow in mist on the star-herder
    Of the glimmering Way.

Light will shine beyond the grim grapple
Of fear for power, while man forever errs,
As in aeons before and after Eden apple
    And the sons of Eve were hers.

Wide awake I lay with my heart quaking,
Feeling the love of the lucky gone before,
While the long relentless surges I heard shaking
    A granite shore.

DEUS

In the clairaudience of dawn
Thou art withdrawn;
In the enormous night sky,
Too far, too high;
But in the anguished mind,
In the heart of despair,
Strangely men find
Thee there.

THE MEMORY

Through languishing light what faint and fading streams
Channel the night — O under dark boughs what dove
Cajoles ? while deep in forest the hunt of dreams
Is color and clamor hushed as the wood is blurred
When the voice of the memory I am dreaming of
      Far off, singing, is heard.

Cadence enchanted, weary not nor fail
Deep in the wood of my heart, like a waterfall
Streaming silver where moon pools are pale,
Torrent whose plash is the innocence of old;
O lovely memory, call and call and call
      Till lips and heart be cold !

THE MUSEUM

For Starr Nelson

An immemorial land
    Here your own.
The brown Egyptian hand
    Graved on stone
With fine relievo line
    Oryx in herds,
Riverhorse, hare,
Design of netted birds.

Earth-red, flat blue,
    Ochre, green,
(Time's sandstorm through)
    Are colors clean.
The ritual people walk
    Profile wise.
They set in the head of the hawk
    Carnelian eyes.

Blood shed by Israelite
    Seeped in sand.
Incredible stars by night
    Lit the black land.
A treasure city white
Between a sphinx's knees.
Pyramid. Valley tomb.
    Pithom.
    Raamses.

Glare and gore.
But line and form we prize.

The full lips move no more,
But the Queen's painted eyes
      Dark and clear
Through eternity stare.
The blowing sand is here.
The light is there.

THE PARALYTIC

Mine was a twisted frame,
    wrenched back and knee,
    before he looked at me
that time he came.

Through matted hair
    with wrinkled features gray,
    beside the dusty way
I lay, and could but stare.

He did not stoop to see,
    nor twitch my rags apart.
    His look lived in my heart
and was a flowering tree.

His look ran in my veins
    like sap, the wine
    exultant of the vine,
and all my pains

flowed from me while I bathed
    in that great light.
    What was my fancied plight ?
I seemed unscathed

by the corrupting pain
    that made me ail.
    I stood up straight and hale
and laughed amain,

laughed to the clutch of tears.
        And still his eyes
        profoundly deep, and wise
with centuries of years

I could not comprehend,
        made me rejoice.
Why ? Then his different voice
said low, "My friend,

our race is not yet run
        against despair and wrath.
        Yours is the planet's path,
and yours to seize the sun,

and deep within the heart
        a universe untrod
        to rule like very God
whereof you are a part."

He held me with his eyes.
        And then he smiled
        as simply as a child.
And on this wise

already I am hence. . . .
        Why do they say,
        who stop beside the way,
"Poor soul !" and drop their pence.

THE VINE

Now is the smell of burning leaves.
And they are casting the branches into the fire.
Always, from childhood, the smell of burning leaves
in an Autumn that grieves.
To what did the vine aspire
that so many reluctant leaves are rustling into the fire ?

There was one vine
higher than beanstalk, taller than laddering light,
into a height
and a new dimension in trine.
And the fruit of the vine ?

Always from childhood the burning leaves
and the pungent blue haze, and the sadness of Autumn days;
scuffling in the gutters the dead leaves.
The good frost smell of Fall, and yet in a season that grieves . . .
Always . . . always. . . .

Bronze ivy on gray wall.
Always in the Fall
I loved the fire colors of the leaves, and the bronze ivy on the
    gray wall.
I loved the gray wall; my hand went over the stone;
I was alone, and the solid buttresses of stone
knew that I was trying, that I was alone
in the desperate sadness of the ballad of Autumn days,
always. . . .

The vine seems
always in my dreams

higher, more branched, more golden, and to climb
up to the doorsill of Time,
though the leaves in their myriads fall.
Vine, vine, whispering vine, high on the infinite wall,
what fruit of the vine ?

But it has been all —
sweet as pomegranate, and bitter — bitter as gall —
it has all been mine.

STUDY OF MAN

Not men as museums !
Such the penmen see.
In the dust and the heat
And the toil of the street
They are other to me.

Men as museums
Abide inside
Skulls of pride,
Dark mausoleums,
Doctrinaire rooms,
Intellectual tombs,
To be deified.

Forever suspect
Pure intellect —
O but throw wide
The gates of the heart
Taking your part
In percipient life
With sweetheart or wife
Or a friend and a friend !

Ever extend
Your boundaries, and be
Inwardly free !
What man is he
They categorize
To a list of lies
While all of their lore
Misses his core,

And still he escapes
In recondite shapes
Who never could yield
To them wholly revealed ?

Men and museums ?
Think not they wed
In the world of the dead
Where the light is instead.
Reach to full height;
Live in that light,
Through the storm and the dread !

Rise on the wings
Of subliminal things;
Go vivid and brief
As the life of the leaf;
Endure, in your love
Of panther and dove,
Laughter and grief !

Men as museums ?
What are they to me ?
Man is an ocean.
I live by the sea.

YOUNG GIRL

Hers the clear brow, the lithe and slender
body, from young proud breasts to feet
that one would think could walk the cloud,
the head held high, the loins too proud
yet for the mastery of surrender,
the lip inviolate and sweet.

This rapt indweller of a dream
where tides of air and tides of ocean,
tides of the blood, and of surmise
that gravely wakens in the eyes,
sway all her flowing grace of motion,
what music has her for its theme ?

An elemental music blended
of earth and sky, of sun and sea,
known only to pristine creation
unsullied by our civilization;
a momentary harmony
bating our excellence pretended.

THE BRIDE

I saw a boy
with wings on his feet,
sudden as joy
in a noisome street
where filthy alleys
festered with lies.
Hills and valleys
were in his eyes.

He sang a woman
wooed of the sky,
her mould no human
shoulder and thigh;
the hilled horizon
her flank and breast.
In snows she lies on
the ranges' crest.

Some deep slow river,
redolent grove,
warm orchard, ever
breathe her love.
Curved upland pasture,
loam for the plough,
these be her vesture;
the sky her brow.

I heard him singing.
I heard him say,
"I shall be bringing
from Her one day

the tilth of greening
and growing field:
the golden meaning,
the starry yield !"

SIREDON

In mountain lakes of Mexico
a larval shape that feeds and breeds
with gills and fins and legs that go
tail-waving through the water-weeds;

a spectre of the spirit, this;
non-evolution's embryo
evading metamorphosis
amorphous yet to come and go

and reproduce its queer condition
as the ephemeris breeds May flies
for larval years, or, formed by fission,
the protozoan multiplies.

Yet *Rudis*, that Earth's prime bequeathes,
when heat beats down and lakes are gone
crawls up the shriveled mud, and breathes,
a small moist lizard on a stone:

The sylph that Paracelsus saw
sparkle and twire within the flame;
the elemental, held in awe;
the salamander's other name;

which, though a little dragon, was
Undine to take a human soul —
symbol of lives wherethrough we pass
till all unformed be formed and whole ?

I saw the lout lurch down the street
with brassy voice and vacant laugh
while round his head all viewless beat
wings of his irised epitaph

because of That whose image he
most grossly was, all formless yet,
who from this element may be
at last to crawl, as, dry from wet,

the newt emerged, that shed its gills
and tiny fins — how changed anon !
May I, O if the Enjoiner wills,
evolve like thee, friend Siredon !

OBITUARY PAGE

Now they begin to go;
the lonely-walking or the crowded-round,
the fortunate, the hapless, friend or foe;
the loosed or bound;
into the dark they flutter, settling slow
like snow upon the ground. . . .

Into the dark, either to depth or height, —
wrenched from convivial tumult, or despair,
in sudden rigor, in that strange despite
of terror, or its foil, delight, —
or inward drawn somewhere
divested of ascension or declension,
moving still near us in some fourth dimension. . . .

No fluttering snow are they, but blades made bare,
plucked from the sheath ! For these I knew were swords
and those were flames — and many were aware,
in age, of that which is not said with words.
O, anywhere,
God fend, and send them into brighter air !

THE GHOST BY NOONDAY

The hovering moment when, in sudden uncanny prevision,
Something within one said, "O now let it never pass !"
As the voices rose and fell, with the clink of cups, and the laught
    But the shadows long on the grass;

Or the moment of breathless meeting; or of impossible parting;
Or the tranced, commingling moment of love's supreme caress,
Hair reckless upon the pillow, the beautiful body breathing
    The passionate yes.

Or the graven moment when in brutal unbearable sorrow
One looked for, and found a bulwark in eyes and a steady mind,
Though the world was stricken void and empty of all tomorrow,
    The precipice blind.

But the other happy times, incredible, transitory
Instants of pure felicity, when the defeated eyes
Were cleansed, the heart exalted; when insupportable glory
    Married surprise.

Was it word or look or likeness, or all of these agreeing,
With knowledge that man is noble, that woman is friend and brav
Ever it cries in the heart that such immediate seeing
    Conquers the grave;

That they return: the mirthful, the ardent, the beautiful people;
That they are there in the sunlight; under the trees, on the lawn;
That their eyes laugh, that they say, "Did you think it could be
    always ?
    "It is !" And are gone.

BIRTH FUNERAL*

" — wee celebrate our own funeralls with cries, even at our birth."

JOHN DONNE

How long ago indeed
Did I begin to die,
Nor held to any creed
For long, though asking why.
The visage that I wore
Was fixed upon a skull;
The dark eyes that implore,
In sockets hard and dull.

I did begin my death
When all my life was sun.
The ending of my breath
My youth could not outrun.
Bay tree was cypress tree
For all my earnest care,
The throbbing flesh of me
A solemn shroud to wear.

But now the dead have given
What Dante's scholar gave,
And strangely from their heaven
One who was once a slave,
Manilius of old,

---

* *Written on receiving a book of thoughts of Latin authors, given in 1885 by Thomas William Parsons to Louise Imogen Guiney.*

27

In Latin strict and pure,
Coins me what's more than gold:
Nascentes morimur.

The end in the beginning !
And I believe, my friend,
That wisdom worth the winning,
Thus won, outshines the end.
For, converse to your truth,
Doth Godhead not engage
I shall renew my youth
When I have shed my age ?

"INFINITE PASSION—"

Dark of the wood. Pungence of Fall.
The sky no wall.
High over all
(a soul's reach, a heart's cry !)
Wintry with stars, the climbing sky
Into the thought
Of the terrible naught,
The God-abyss. . . .

Here on a fleck of turning ground,
Ocean's profound Odyssean sound.
This life . . . This . . .

Grate-grind, grate-grind, I heard a cricket
In the critical thicket.

OUTLANDER

He came a star-roamer
From a cold fiery clime.
He sang, a young Homer,
Down dark streets of time,
His brow scarred by lightning,
His lip curled to bliss,
His forest eyes frightening
A sham world like this.

He crouched by the ocean
And strummed a deep stave.
The pinewood in motion
Stepped down to the wave.
The glassed wave reared swinging
Its mantle foam-free,
Spellbound by that singing,
The fanged cobra sea.

The sun's pennoned glory
Wrought pageants of sky.
The dark promontory
Flung a white gull on high.
He sang golden-throated
Sidereal rhyme
Of chaos world-moted
And the dream we call time.

When lamps lit the village
He strolled through moon-shade.
Their trawling and tillage
He hummed, and their trade.

They turned, craning after,
Then near or afar
Followed jostling with laughter
His lilting guitar.

By the green and the churches
He swerved up the hill.
He climbed as one searches
A cynosure still,
Till high above steeple,
Branch-black on the moon,
He turned toward the people
And plucked forth a tune.

They saw Borealis,
They saw comets fly.
Dream pasture, dream palace
Stood clear in the sky.
A deep chord was aching
To tears in each breast.
A great wave was breaking
And thundering to rest.

No later revealing
Quite made it come right
As to why they were kneeling
On Hill Street that night.
They scrambled up, dusting
Their knees, and stood still.
They coughed, looked mistrusting,
Then gazed up the hill.

Yet no one felt sillier,
No soul found it vain,

Now all things familiar
Rushed round them again.
Over orchard and arbor
A star trailed and fell.
The height above the harbor
Said softly, farewell.

VICTORY

Have you looked on the dead?

In that composure
with no disclosure
of hope or dread,
that strict quiet
under the fiat,
all is said.

Have you searched the face
with tears burning,
with wrung yearning,
the features pale,
past assail,
of grave grace?

Babble of words, chatter of print,
whine of envy, battle-dint
of anger, bluster of power,
where are they heard? Like spray they fall
from a rock wall.
Stamped in the mint
of the ageless now
lip, eyelid, brow
in the still hour.

Rage as we will,
faintly the while
the dead smile,
lying so still.

II

THE NOBLEST FRAILTY

"And love's the noblest frailty of the mind."
DRYDEN : *THE INDIAN EMPEROR*

TOKEN

For M. F. B.

Why do I love you,
For I love you truly ?
Why do you love me ?
Who am I to say ?
Well we know the ruffled wing,
The tossed mane unruly,
Wild nature's way.

First for your foibles,
Curiously endearing;
Next for your kindnesses
Such as angels' be;
Last, in the forest,
For the sun-chequered clearing
You are to me.

Yes, we are lucky.
(Speak not what is given;
The charm against mischief,
Hide it in your heart !)
Birds in our high elms
Run roulades of heaven.
The sea holds a part.

All that I know is
It was someone's doing
When the night was darkest,
When the hour was late.

You were the end
Of blundering and pursuing.
You smiled at fate.

Why do I love you ?
Is it any wonder —
You who say forever,
On the way that I am drawn,
No, to the lightning;
Sorry, to the thunder;
Yes, to the dawn.

ECHO

She was beautiful   Why ?
For her sloped budding breast,
silver thigh ?

She was beautiful   Yes
for these and more intimate things . . .
as, the nape whence the tendrilled hair springs,
the disarming tress. . . .

She was beautiful   These
were her beauties . . .
white throat   taut knees

a clear deerlike grace
proud chin   still face

and her satin and steel. . . .
She was all bells in peal
she was all hounds in chase
clouds in lace. . . .

She was beautiful   Why ?
For the distance profound
in her falconlike eye
where the lights of Atlantis were drowned. . . .

She was beautiful   When ?

Ah, lustra agone
when the moon of her mind
shone
on men. . . .

THE FOREST

From Beaulieu Heath to Hampworth Common
    Great oaks and beeches grow.
There lived all beauty in one woman
    A lifetime's time ago.

From Salisbury to Southampton Water
    By No Man's Land you go.
There the birch grew a silver daughter
    Where there was none to know.

'Twixt Burley Beacon and Allum Green
    Apostle oak-trees stood,
But dwined long gone, and few were seen
    When a queen walked in the wood.

But a golden eagle saw I there,
    A merlin and a dove;
O, were they birds that winged the air,
    Or images of love ?

Know you the crimson underwing,
    Or Burley of the bees,
Green oakbloom honey, gold wasps that sting,
    White ghost-owls in the trees ?

If you know charcoal-burners' huts
    And the gipsy caravan,
Wild pony hooves, gray rabbit scuts,
    You'll know where the daemon ran.

Behind a screen of scrub and furze
    A thread of smoke twines blue.
The dream of a forest house was hers
    In a fairytale come true.

Ytene they called that furzy waste
    Of old; the wood they ward;
For a seedling oak grows not in haste.
    Hollies and haws must guard.

But love was all too swift to burn
    Before the leaves were gay.
In mossy sward, and bracken and fern,
    The heart is wiled away.

The green had covered the blackthorn's veil,
    The bracken stood too high,
The caterpillar left his trail,
    Myriad the forest fly.

I knew it not in earlier spring
    Snow-white on either hand,
With blossom shed on heather and ling —
    But I knew Broceliande.

For a heron stood beside a stream,
    A turquoise butterfly
Flitted the glade through gleam and gleam
    And melted in the sky.

Where Lyndhurst rules the roads that trace
    Northward or south and west
The birch trees leaned in silver grace,
    The Graces she loved best.

And Beaulieu's witch of rides and *landes*
    Slept soft, nor lifted head,
Though the pond where Tyrrell washed his hands
    With Norman blood was red.

That witch's name was Mary Dove,
    Buried with the barrowed urn;
A true name to delight my love
    Whose foot scarce pressed the fern;

Though a road may lead from Stoney Cross
    To a mound on Fritham Plain,
But the road to where I knew my loss
    I'll never find again.

Nor is there word in Domesday Book
    For all the things I know,
Who felt how hazel eyes could look,
    A lifetime's time ago.

Wild plum its feathery whiteness throws
    On the cruel winds of Spring.
Where the wood is purple-black as sloes,
    Holly and ivy cling.

Bluebells and wood-anemones
    And foxgloves by the stream,
A slender girl could gather these
    Like the lilies of a dream.

When the autumn fern-cutter piles his cart
    With bracken brown and red,
From mist and frost that chill the heart
    Looks forth the lovely dead.

From upland heath to Solent side
    The forest breathes my loss;
Nor Lyndhurst knows my silver bride,
    Deer-Leap to Lady Cross.

Like a soft and covered woodland track,
    Like a buried river's flow,
Delight, despair come quivering back
    From a lifetime's time ago.

LOVE'S MIRTH REMEMBERED

With your wise childishness,
once, when I laughed, you said
in partly feigned distress
and mild surprise,
"Why are you laughing ?"
and gazed with great round eyes
and high proud head.

I knew, looking at you,
why I was laughing. It was my duty.
Such quivering fire; so much delicate beauty;
reason *perdu* !

As in high summer
among the gleaming grasses
some sorrowful soul and proud
hearing a meadow-lark ripple as he passes
might lift his throat to the azure
pierced by keen pleasure
and laugh to the cloud,

so I
for wonder of your dower
of unconscious art
in loveliness, your wayward innocent power
that shook my heart.

Yes, I laughed, I believe
because of the miraculous men despair to
find, unpremeditation clear as dew.
Grieve not, if you do grieve !
Why, all the while you knew I should never dare to
laugh at you !

COMMUNION

First a forest
dark as despair.
I battled gasping,
grasping air . . .
burst to a clearing.
   You were there.

Horror and anguish,
blood, filth, pain
made of my being
visible stain.
I fell before you.
   I was fain

Of calm and cool,
of light and bright,
as to thirst a pool,
to a clamberer height,
air to the fool
with the forest to fight.

The moon in a veil
mounted haze:
monstrance pale
with nimbus of rays,
as though at some rail
of prayer and praise

I knelt. It seemed
a grail in the mist.

My spirit dreamed
eucharist.
Moonrays streamed,
air was whist. . . .

The dream passed.
Sun shed
day at last
on my bed.
Fact bound fast.
You were dead.

VISITATION

I have wronged you deeper than they know,
      being maddened by you;
though not one thing they have said is so
      who would decry you.

A tall and winding ivory stair
      in a tower you are
to dark night, and wine of air
      and a weeping star.

Lullaby low your voice runs.
      Your wise breast
is deep with hidden moons or suns
      of strange rest;

yet absent with the speed of light
      your presence is;
wherefrom I only judge the height
      by the abyss.

Thus of this scroll I make an end
      who am slow to learn,
yet thereunto a name have penned
      as wrote Traherne.

"DESINE, DULCIUM MATER SAEVA CUPIDINUM"

. . . Then one white arm above her head she tossed,
like snowdrift lying pale and looking lost,
sighing with lowered lids, as Love forbore,
"Nay, now, dear love, no more !"

Trancelike that hour when languor's supersession
lulled into dream the passion of possession,
rage of the lion subsiding to the deep
of pure and lamblike sleep,

whereto, weighed in the scales of earth and heaven,
the divinitive and moonset crown is given
even as the red heart on Love's brows hath set
a darker carcanet,

like the Pharaonic headdress red and white.
So Love, the cruel empress, rules the night,
in tyrant ferment of the vein and brain
to claim her suzerain,

and on foundation of mere flesh and blood
raiseth the soul to fiery hardihood,
while out of grievous sighs and sobbing breath
devotion conquers death. . . .

THE JEST

Accept the jest,
and laugh because I love you !
Only the best
I ever wanted of you.

That being too dear,
impetuously discarded,
it would appear
I am the more regarded.

As to who wins
or anyone that loses,
choice of our sins
a kindly God refuses.

Maugre desire
through which we met and parted —
a sullen fire ! —
we go the more light-hearted.

But, Heaven or Hell,
my better love be round you;
for I know well
you are as first I found you

in charm and zest.
How many stand above you ?
Take then the jest
and laugh because I love you !

SONG HEARD IN SLEEP

High above hill and valley my love and I did meet
        a long time ago.
She held me to her bosom, and O I found it sweet,
        and the wind blowing softly and slow.

High above hill and valley my love and I did say
        a long time ago,
"I will love you truly forever and a day !"
        and the wind blowing softly and slow.

High above hill and valley my love and I did part
        a long time ago.
Tears rained down from heaven as we lay heart to heart,
        and the wind blowing softly and slow.

High above hill and valley my love and I do fare
        and all things we know.
With new love and wonder we glide the glowing air,
        and the wind blowing softly and slow.

III

GALLERY

MARSYAS IN AUTUMN

Her who won Athens from the Sea
and wove the contest on her loom,
the teasing god of love in glee
saw make her wisdom's mouth assume
such humorous aspect on the flute
it dropped from her tormented hand
to where, half human and half brute,
the satyr roamed the autumn land
and spied it through the embered leaves
adrift beneath the umber trees,
and with a sound like one who grieves
knelt down to it on shaggy knees,
pursed his own ignorant lips, and made
what all the woodland crept to hear,
wild music that a god waylaid,
flayed in the fiery fading year.

MASS FOR THE DEAD

"About midnight he suddenly sat up and looked aroun
him with dull, non-seeing eyes. . . ."

ERNEST NEWMAN ON THE DEATH OF MOZA

"But in the great artist of genius there is also another pr
totype, which, in the case of musicians, I may best define
calling it, not the love of God, but the love of the God
Music. . . . And just as God loves those who love Hi
so Music loves those who are its true lovers and showe
its riches upon them. Finally — and most mysterious of
— there is some hidden connection in great musical geni
between the love of God and this love of the God
Music. The one enriches the other as if there were a ma
riage between them."

W. J. TURNER: "MOZART: THE MAN AND HIS WORK

This is the second time that you have come,
Tall, thin and dark, a dark man dressed in gray;
And you will come again, and I will lie
In the rain, in the rain alone, in the seething rain
That makes mud of the clay. You offer me
Gold, do you say? The only gold I've had
Was of the spirit, the demoniacal
Power I had of the melodic mind,
The infinite resource whence I could summon
Masses, concertos, symphonies, sonatas,
Cantatas, oratorios, fantasias;
Each instrument in the polyphonic scheme
At its fit function; and, for harmony,
Between the upper instruments and the bass,
The figuring of the delicate harpsichord;
Power to demonstrate in the sonata,
In length of movement, in breadth of my design,

54

All I had learned from Haydn, freeing rhythm,
Deepening, till the profound experience
Of composition, that seemed to suckle me,
Enlarged the form and the resourcefulness
Of every instrument; enlarged the scale;
Until in the C Minor Mass I pressed
Up toward the polyphonic peak, the singing
Consummation of all the vehemence
And drama in me, under long control,
Flowerlike unfolding — and the movement rose
And rose, and trembled close to the sublime,
Yet failed of the finale I had dreamed,
Twisting cool and light, reluctant from the height
Where one, surpassing Palestrina's rapture,
Will one day rule, sombrely. Ah, much power
I have, but not that power, not as yet !
Though, silent auditor, when you come again
(And you will come again, as first you came
When I was finishing Die Zauberflöte,
And asked a Requiem, and gave me gold !)
Why, when you come again, who knows but I
May have advanced beyond my melodies
And beyond moonlight on Vienna roofs
To summon more than a mere ghostly statue
Of a grotesque romance. I see you there,
The very — the very what ? What is it, Constance,
I sought in Aloysia and in you
And my own soul ? When what we sought was gold,
The world frustrated what God alone refines.
Destiny tolls. Those are no magic chimes
From our cathedral bells, though I had thought them
Our own St. Peter's. There was nothing magic
In penury, to assuage my own good Kaiser
When I resigned my office, and composed

Immortal deliciousness for an absurd
And stupid tale. There is no magic flute
To play away the fiend Hieronymus,
That devil's changeling for my dear archbishop,
Or to avenge gross insult, find me lodgings
Or pupils in an inimical Vienna,
Till, to make tour, perforce I pawned my plate.
And yet, in spite of jealousy and fury
The luck changed, and the famous abbé brought me
My theme from Beaumarchais. And, once again,
Da Ponte challenged me with Don Giovanni
To match my Figaro, whose Cherubino
Compacted all my youth. So, though Vienna
At every window, on each crooked corner,
Glancing askance leered, waiting for my fall,
Prague stormed applause; and, again, stormed applause
Even when a valet's elusive nimbleness
Was superseded by the heavy tread
Of the inexorable dead. . . . The hands,
Cold marble hands, lay hold !

                                        I am not old
Nor was I truly young. But born of beauty
Into a golden infancy, who toured
Through courts and cities, with powdered wig and sword
Seated at the covered keyboard, improvising
For harpsichord or organ; at Versailles
Played to the stately aging Pompadour
The clavier gilt and lacquered; by packet-boat
From Calais, to the Hanoverian king,
And at Spring Gardens and St. James's Park;
In Paris, quick with the romantic spirit
Fed by Rousseau; and saw the tricks and farces,
Harlequinades and other devil's antics
The Viennese intellectuals applaud,

While the variety within my brain,
A coruscation of color all in sound,
Took ardor from the heart, brilliance and glamour
From my high spirits and my bubbling youth,
Till gorgeous humor of a pantomime
Blent with morality veiled in allegory
Of the brotherhood of the Great Architect,
Yet, flashing satire, drew me swiftly on
To poisoned fame. You ask a Requiem now ?
Am I Sebastian Bach ? In Eisenach,
The Minnesingers' town, there grew a power
Profound, sublime, mounting to the chorale
That cried, O come sweet death ! You, in the shadow;
You, darkling by the door; you, where the moonlight
Seems to shine through you — are you hooded there ?
Why do you stand so still ? And did you ask me
To write a requiem ? I have written many
Concertos, masses, symphonies and sonatas,
Cantatas, oratorios. . . . Ah, God,
I babble, I am hunger-faint, more chill
Than the saint's cavern in the Mönchsberg, —
Than when, the night before my Don Giovanni
(Death in my Quintet — my father's death between —
And now this vision of death more complete !)
I labored writing down the overture
That like a roiling fever filled my brain,
While, to aid wakefulness, my Constance fed me
A brittle sugar-froth of fairy-tales
Laughingly told; and thus, while Cinderella
Lost the glass slipper, I measured out the tread
Relentless of my statue; till, indeed,
The memory that had held the *Miserere*
Of the Sistine, to be note by note transcribed,
Failed me not, and I finished as the morning

Grayed into sun. . . . You there, are you a shadow
Or are you man? I feel upon my forehead
The seething rain. I know my body lifted
And borne . . . St. Mary's cemetery knows
The paupers' plot. . . . My friends can go no further.
The wind-blown rain is weeping; the rain is tears. . . .
Johann Chrisostom Wolfgang Amadeus
Sigismund Mozart, to Maria Anna,
Mother and sister . . . and to all my friends. . . .
And so, the last grand tour. . . . Borrowing time!
The tempo rubato in an adagio
With the left hand — thus — measuring the time!
Mannheim and Paris, Munich, and back to Salzburg. . . .
I am exhausted, and I cannot drive
Away the picture of that unknown man.
Yet though it be in penury I die
Lost and alone, twice he has come and paid
This certain sum. It is not for my soul,
Though never have I known what man he was.
But can you hear it now? For now, at last,
It throngs in me; and all the instruments
Are filled with manifestation of a god
Who never yet has failed me, even when
I wrote adagio for a glass harmonica,
Fantasia for a clock! Creative heaven
At the piano-forte, through the night
Like a still water, when the whole wealth of tones
Welled inexhaustible! The music lifts,
It climbs, it marches, advances on the height
Where at the last it will not fail me now.
For all my childhood comprehended, all
That gave me golden youth, a golden spur,
Pours through me from the superhuman source,
Fount of the stars, chaos that formed the Word,

Greatening and deepening, till every rhythm
And the full resonance of each instrument
Presses toward tragedy, up toward victory,
Toward exaltation beyond the cruel grave,
Toward love, toward love. . . . And the deserted graveyard
Trodden and sodden with the gusts of rain,
The pauper's place forsaken and forgotten,
There they will never find me, never now.

EMINENCE ROUGE

When Richelieu rode, incarnate France,
Past crumbled castle, humbled town,
Blue armor did his cope enhance,
With all of Rohan's strongholds down.
The nobles and the magistrates
Bowed low before their open gates,
And he, the favorite of the fates,
Wore more than mitre, crest, or crown.

Bishops and princes in his train
Followed with fawning zeal to please.
The Empire knew his power, and Spain;
The Rhone unto the Pyrenees.
From La Rochelle and Montauban
The last brave Huguenot hope was gone;
And puffing forth with haste anon
The city fathers brought their keys.

Twelve thousand horsemen trampling dust
Shook far-off England with their tread.
The stammering Louis vowed his trust.
The Catholic star blazed overhead.
Where recreant Condé slew in haste,
Cruel d'Estrees laid the country waste,
Provence and Languedoc defaced,
Their townsmen galley-slaves or dead.

Between the Italian and her son,
The Hapsburg gloom, the Bourbon spite,
With brilliant moves the board was won,
Hatred or weakness lending light.

On firelit walls within his room
The menace of the court might loom,
Yet wither ashen in the gloom
While still his fever rose to fight.

For fire was in that countenance, fined
To mastery of violent men,
And there was greatness in that mind
(Parchment-corrosive on his pen !)
And though the flesh its frailness knew,
The intellect burned clearly through
The sallow mask. His spirit grew
The realm's eternal watch-tower then.

Protestant, Catholic, men of God,
Raged at this eminence, and died;
For wheresoever Armand trod
A further faith he made his guide.
Past Jesuit and Huguenot,
Guise plot and Condé counterplot,
A national state his thought begot.
All else extrinsic seemed beside.

He used the heretic, he used
Whatever instrument could cope
With Hapsburg power; shrewdly fused
Strange elements; he used the Pope.
When greatness of the Golden King
Caused jangled German bells to ring,
His policy was action's spring,
He was a nation's single hope.

Armored in ice, but in the dyes
Of Sardanapalus attired,

With onyx softer than his eyes,
And by one sole ambition fired,
The intrigues of a court depraved,
The tigerish lords, a queen that raved,
A wavering king, his pathway paved
Toward the illusion he desired.

And if, on all that he destroyed
He builded what he might not scan
With the enlightenment enjoyed
So briefly since by modern man,
Past dynasties he saw a state
If absolute yet somehow great;
And all the gambits of his fate
He met with craft Cartesian.

He watched besieging ocean shine
On a dead city, and thunder doom;
The Pyrenees, the Alps, the Rhine,
Flanders, he saw in thunder loom.
Each through his nature played their part:
The tyrant and the man of art.
The France he guarded in his heart
Burns like a sunset on his tomb.

THE RIDE TO THE DANUBE

Lord of the World he may be ! But the hooves strike fire
From the dust of the road to the pace of headlong desire
Plunging on from Olympia's gates, though the heart be torn
And throb in a body already wasted and worn,
And a boy of twenty, through streets of Paris who ran
Begging aid in the cause of Christendom, ride like a man
Though the Rhine be barred, while the couriers of the King
On all roads make the flint from the flying fetlock ring;
Though, at Frankfort, Armand, that other Prince of the Blood,
Turn back, as the galloping gentleman splashed with mud
Tenders the letter sealed with the Royal seals —
Lord of the World he may be ! But the road unreels,
And a thousand gulden and one diamond ring
May yet outface the unseeing stare of a King
Condemning a mother to exile and spurning the son. . . .
There is the Danube, when all is said and done;
There shines the river ! The Crescent against the Crown
Shall ebb like a tide as the horse-tail hordes go down.
For the sad cavalier, with destiny pale in his face,
Like a twisted ape in black rides a hammering race,
Since under Vienna ramparts the Turkish mine
Explodes with smoke to eclipse man's hope in trine.

Recall the patched soutane and the tarnished shoes;
But the Little Abbé rides with nothing to lose.
From the Sun King's shadow, his idol a brief time since,
Recklessly rides a penniless vagabond prince —
For the god with the gilded wreath and the high curled head
Is a sounding brass, and the worshipful love is dead
For an empty Louis, a bloated popinjay man. . . .
Savoy rides now, and Soissons, and Carignan,

Though an Emperor's troops retire and an Emperor flee,
And the Turk come on like the limitless waves of the sea
To foam at Vienna walls, as the ocean swells
Endlessly effluent through the Dardanelles;
Though the janizaries and Tartar tribes be here
And cruel Kara Mustapha, the Grand Vizier —
That the spate of the East be stemmed, that the West may live
Rides now the derided, the outcast, the fugitive !

Ride into the years, Eugene, when the world shall hark
The tread of your armies against the Grand Monarque,
When the Prince (at Passau unwanted, without a corps)
Shall with Marlborough move to the forefront of the war —
From Turin, from Oudenarde, with fame on the wing,
Against a tyrant and an absolute king,
Until that day when, as to a trumpet peal,
To the strong Allies falls the citadel of Lille ! . . .
Louis defeated, and now Olympia gone,
And wolflike winter, and war still lingering on,
And tiger summer, and last that bloodiest day
And night of battle and loss called Malplaquet. . . .
Then, builded of mist, behold a mightier scene
Of night attack, grey fog rolling between;
The Turk surprised, the rush of the grenadiers
To the battery-mound, the heights taken, the cheers
That shook Belgrade. . . . Then the final ride of the plain
Retraversing the field of the long campaign
Past where (When began this ride !) the brother fell. . . .
And, far behind, hear the soldier voices swell
To the song of Eugene, as, with sombre eyes downcast
And deathlike immobile face, and, to the last,
The shoulder hunched in the plain worn coat of brown,
He rides to salvos in through his Austrian town,
That rare Vienna. . . . But even as he began,

No palace nor pleasaunce can hold the man,
Though all be grandeur — rare garden grafts nor scions,
Macaws nor golden eagles nor apes and lions,
Engravings, fire-screens wrought of ormolu,
Venetian mirrors, nor books that Leibnitz knew,
Nor gold and silver brocade of metallic shine. . . .
He rides to his last campaign along the Rhine
With a Frederick, newly-risen, to know what skill
Of strategy still may be shaped by a master will
Though at last too late to win. . . .
                              But now the road
Rings to a charger's clatter, close-bestrode
By a hunched frailty, a simian dwarf of a man —
And Savoy is riding, Soissons, and Carignan;
And a boy is riding, a young voice sobbing in ire,
"Lord of the World he may be — !"
                              How the hooves strike fire !

TO A CAROLINE KNIGHT

Red-haired Jack Suckling, often seen
At Peccadillo bowling green,
Who coated a whole troops of carls
In white and scarlet for King Charles
And plumed them like the popinjay,
Against the Scots that ran away !

O tuneful Jack, without a care
In midnight revels at the *Bear*,
To Lovelace friend and wild Carew;
Town blade and theologian too;
Fighter at Leipzic with Gustavus;
And at the cards and dice, God save us!

The "brisk round eye," red face and nose,
The perked-up beard, the bright court clothes;
For poem piquant or playful letter
Or daring wager, where a better ?
Who bowled with skill at Tunbridge Wells,
Then skipped away to something else.

No Digby's cudgel can undo
The warm regard I feel for you
Who "prized black eyes" and feats at bowls
More than crowned poets or pious souls;
Who scattered gold and scoffed at bays;
Whose plays were bad, whose poems were plays.

Who led his friends a morris dance;
Who fled from Parliament to France;
Found Stuarts faithless; and at last

From mockery to poison passed;
In singing metric how adroit !
Always peculiar, and a poet —

For still in air your verses hover
Of "Why so pale and wan, fond lover ?"
And "Time shall moult away his wings"
Ere such another amorist sings,
While Castaly its dew is shedding
Upon your Ballad of a Wedding.

A jester at the Inn of Art,
Satirist with a buoyant heart,
Who found a lady, 'spite her smiles,
"False as the tears of crocodiles,"
And, flouter of the almanack,
Saw great rare Ben drink sherris sack,

Those who incline to crib and peg,
Are they aware you well might beg
Indulgence as their game's inventor ?
Gamester Sir John, you stand our mentor
In wit and wine; so, with no truckling,
Here's to your merry ghost, great Suckling !

The red roofs are glowing above the slow water
    of cool-flowing Tyne.
The kirkyard is showing where Haddington's daughter
    has lain lang syne.

And yet, by contraries, there rots in St. Mary's
    the skull's aventail
of Charles' coadjutor, that red persecutor
    the grim Lauderdale.

O gallant Jean Baillie, in youth you went gaily
    who met in the High
the grim one we reckon exalts Ecclefechan
    through thunders of sky.

You faced, at your station, neglect and privation
    with power of the mind,
and showed how those sages who curse through the ages
    rely on your kind.

Enduring and human your wit of a woman
    and grace of a girl —
but rotten his plot in and mouldering forgotten
    the bones of the Earl !

Through "killing time" 's stour he stormed in his power
    "the man was the law."
The Tolbooth was looming, the doomster was glooming,
    the Maiden spread awe.

By craft murder-minded all justice was blinded —
     by party, by power.
He raged and he harried; and horror was married
     to law in that hour.

Yet Tyne is a river that washes forever
     the fever from fires;
the Lammermuirs rolling to southward, extolling
     the jewel of the shires.

Nor least of its glory one Scotchwoman's story:
     from vehemence and spleen
in life never parted: the pawky, high-hearted,
     unparalleled Jean !

Rain on the plane trees, and his spirit gone
To dream with Phidias in the Parthenon;
For Aesculapius an empty eye
And the stone edifice of Thomas Guy.
Snow falling on the River, and its fleece
In Southwark raising images of Greece
Chryselephantine: ivory, gold, and rose.
Thus, burning through dark London's fogs and snows,
Or high in Hampstead, with the summer heats,
The vase of fire that was the soul of Keats.

"THERE FELL THY SHADOW"

Mesmerized eye in Conder's portrait,
rictus of anguish, chin leaned on
cupped hand, like Keats; but profile saying,
"What did Keats see in Fanny Brawne ?"

Innocent restaurant madonna.
Poland's Propertius, half-dismayed,
nursing a mortal immortal passion,
playing halma with Adelaide.

At a bar-table's slab of marble
(Noisy Shaftesbury Avenue !)
scraps of paper, a stub of pencil,
serpentine green absinthe or two.

Glimmering reach of endless evening;
after Bridge Dock, and flaring nights
blotting warehouse and black starred water,
streaming torches and struggling lights.

Odd Pierrot to a child of moonlight !
Soho's miasma drawing from air
(Half through "Missie" and half Horatian)
litany of all youth's despair.

One in their psychic veiling symbols,
virginal worship, echoing tomb;
out of his river of lights in darkness
Cynara sighing to Ulalume.

SOLDIER

My father was a soldier; he obeyed
what others, wrong too often, had to say;
and when he was afraid, he was afraid
    in a stern lonely way.

The speculation of his eagle mind
hovered above their ignorance of him;
and he was just and generous and kind
    and whimsical and grim.

He had an erudition hard to match,
a pride upon whose point he often ran,
quicksilver wisdom difficult to catch,
    the ironic mask of Man,

the eye austere, the tart and witty tongue,
the thought that knew men's actions all unsure;
but even in age his heart was warm and young
    and his intention pure.

About his mouth there was a smiling hid
that gorgon death could never turn to stone;
and when they lowered down the coffin lid
    I heard a trumpet blown.

BERGAMOT

*To the Old World, a perfume; to the New World,
the Prairie Rose **

You have seen white-hooded conestogas go
Pitching like boats across the prairie waves;
Known the hoof-trampling of the buffalo;
Have nodded over plainsmen's shallow graves;
Have watched the snowy uprolling summer cloud
In huge blue heaven; have spoken home to those
With rifle forearm-cradled, eagle-proud,
      Striding to find
        the western rose.

You have heard the rattler on the rock in air,
Belltail crotalus with lightning in his tongue;
Seen wild ass batter stallion for his mare,
Flustered brown partridge scuttling with her young;
Prairie-dog villages with owl and snake,
Cottonwood coulee marked by the hangman's tree,
Skull-whitened trails the longhorns used to take;
      Assiniboine;
        wild Pawnee.

You knew Chief Joseph, Homer might have sung;
The Little Big Horn, where our troopers died;
How farms reached west, though Sioux and Osage clung
While white men battled toward the Great Divide;
And still, as lover of Ocean feels the blue,

* My identification of bergamot as the western rose has been
intelligently disputed. It remains a symbol to me. Wild Bergamot
is meant, and not "Oswego Tea" or "Bee Balm." Wild Bergamot is
found from Maine to Minnesota and from Florida to Kansas.

73

Far inland, all its deep domain disclose
At one salt touch, ever our West through you
      Breathed bergamot,
          the prairie rose!

The Arkansas you knew, and knew the Platte.
Your grass was surf against the arid Plains.
Homesteaders trooping down the dusty flat,
Traders and trappers flanking wagon-trains.
Through the long valleys the cavalcade and load,
Sunbonnet under tilt, with child at breast;
Fringed leggin's on the raw-boned mounts they rode —
      The new abode
          moved ever west;

The west of bloodied sunset, streamered dawn
On grasslands vast and distance dwindling far,
Cloud-towered mirage in violet haze withdrawn
And wagons rolling toward a sundown star;
Up Rockies, Sierras, as the hunters go,
Till on some summit, high among the snows,
Aloof, gigantic, the Form that all men know
      Chilled in their breast
          the western rose.

Who sees your pungent clusters in the sage
Where now the rusty bundled cars rock by,
Or the high thundering truck declares the Age,
Or the long freight crawls upward toward the sky, —
Who knows your heart, past petals, bracts, and leaves,
The greater part of this our country knows,
And why our western wind exults — and grieves —
      with bergamot
          our prairie rose.

74

Where towers of glass and steel and stone
        stand keep and barbican
of those who rule our toil and own
        miner and artisan,
factory worker and engineer,
stevedore, clerk, artificere,
drudge and plodder who persevere,
press, law, science in every sphere,
there falls the shadow of the pioneer,
the shadow of the mountain man.

Circassian walnut, marble, chrome,
        rich textures from Iran
adorn each girdered honeycomb
        where suave directors plan.
Obsequious hush that fills such fanes,
white bowls of light on golden chains,
far from loud shops and travelling cranes,
soothe the prodigious guiding brains. . . .
So what, in all this ease, explains
the shadow of the mountain man ?

The Rockies knew the buckskin breed,
        (Kit Carson was their best.)
tracker and trapper of Nimrod's seed
        through ranges of the west.
The Southwest felt his lack of law,
Bent's trading fort on the Arkansaw;
"The white gals is too 'fofarraw.'
I'll strike for Taos and trap a squaw !"
Never a Navajo could awe
the fire that filled his breast.

He was barbarous, drunken, hell on a spree
      with the Cheyenne and the Sioux.
He knew Ute lodges and Pawnee,
      and he liked the varmints too.
To the carcajou and the rattlesnake
he was kin, but loved Kaintuck hoe-cake.
No Greaser's sass he'd ever take,
but he pranced the real fandango shake,
and for sweet sad songs his heart could ache;
and he pushed his contracts through.

He climbed with Jedediah Smith
      as they crested the Divide,
or Becknell did he travel with,
      or Frémont, in his pride ?
The merchants traded, the merchants made
fortunes in furs and the fabrics trade.
Keelboats of goods the streams essayed.
The teamsters battled Injun raid
on the Pittsburgh wagon-cavalcade,
and sprawled to the sands and died.

Ramrod and pouch and powder-horn,
      So quaint to the business mind !
So long ago was a free man born
      who sought what he could find !
Long-haired, sun-tanned, and tough to the bone,
his animals died on the Cimarron.
With pack and trap-sack, all alone
he strove where the whirling snow is blown
to scourge Sierra and Yaller Stone
as the farthest trails go blind.

So he cradles his rifled "two-shoot" gun,
  and carved of bronze he stands,
from the flats where the elk and buffler run,
  from the stream-fed beaver lands,
with peltries at six dollars a plew,
and a rifle, cocked for an interview,
that throws plumb-centre; a bowie too
that's tickled the hump-ribs of a few.
He could lift your hair and count his coup
on a thumb of his horny hands.

"I've trapped in heaven an' airth an' hell,"
  says a voice in the grizzled jaws,
"An' a putrified forest I seed as well,
  an' wrenched off a black b'ar's claws.
When the bitin' gale blew up in the rocks,
we et the parflesh off'n our moc's,
an' the city fellers in fustian frocks
woulda fell an' died at our horses' hocks,
fer at last, we was chewin' our rifle stocks
like a stump thet th' beaver gnaws !"

But now we are highly civilized.
  Kit Carson's kind are dead.
And rich with oil, and much surprised,
  is some once hostile red.
Now we are powerful ! All the nations
hail our production with oblations.
We are fed and clothed by corporations
who from our need wring high occasions
for gorgeous profits and large elations . . .
And the world's end's overhead.

He would say, "rubbed out," in the words he knew.
     (The shadow shoots up a span.)
He knew Green River, he knew Big Blue,
     he knew where the great herds ran . . .
So chain men down to pillar and pier
of your towers that soar to the stratosphere !
You can buy and sell them, year on year,
with your goods and your gold and your trumpery gear,
but the shadow waits — and the shadow's here —
the shadow of the mountain man !

CHILD OF THE WORD

O child, I will remember how the word
Bloomed in your delicate voice distinct and true,
The rose's velvet with its gauze of dew,
The name in Eden for the first time heard;
To our astonishment how you averred
More of the deadly nightshade than you knew;
How on your lip the wonder of language grew
Till our rough tongue took flute-notes of a bird.

In curls and eyes the teasing of a sprite;
Pronunciation rendering age as moony as
A lad intoxicated with his love,
Since I discerned, in all you babbled of,
The exquisite satisfaction, grave delight
With which your small mouth syllabled, "Petunias !"

TO RIDGELY TORRENCE

You of our time, and chiefly in our time
sign of the incorruptible in art;
aloof when many all too gladly run
down a steep place, whose name of old was Legion,
the unclean spirits potent to possess
only the snorting herd upon the mountains;
you in our time nor ever of our time
but, as you were at first, artificer
of a clean art, a strict, and a humane;
and the remembrancer of gentle greatness
that walked our city of sorrows long ago;
you of the little, but that little best,
the grape that spills a wine upon the tongue
ripened on Helicon; you of the quiet
meditation, and deeply graven thought —
here, in an evening of the lamp, I lift
a ghostly chalice to your ever kind
and lively countenance, and to your words
that spirit the iris out of air, and carve
the Corinthian acanthus in the stone.

FEE SIMPLE

In Memory of C. E. S. W.

"By what right," my old friend said,
    who is dead,
"By what right of man does he
territory hold in fee
because by fight or fraud or chance,
or shrewd dealing of the dead,
the law calls an inheritance
what should revert to all instead ?
Such land as lords, in days ere this
held in feudal benefice.
Absolute or qualified
by precedent or apothegm
still the great estates abide
with those, however good they be,
who never lifted hand for them
or paid one penny of the fee,
while in our cities slum on slum
jeer against millennium,
and the landlord, and the brain
avaricious, still distrain
God's own people in their pain !"

He was a splendid Jovelike man
with white beard and lion mane,
long a lion of the law
where his voice and mien could awe;
once a soldier of the plain;
and the bullseye often hit
with a Rabelaisian wit,

and the cantharus he knew
cheering Bacchus and his crew
with Caecubam. Beauty too
of the poet heart of Man,
Attic and American;
Who would have been a friend at ease
with lyric Aristophanes
or Socrates or Pericles.
From his vineyard hills he saw
the lampadrome of stars by night
overwhelming all our law
from the source and core of light,
and all the fruits of earth he knew,
and love at its most lovely height.
Hale and young and brave and true,
what he knows in space and time
where the truth is luminous,
through his wit and in his rhyme
glimmeringly descends to us,
lavishly beyond mischance,
our great unearned inheritance.

She was all fire and spirit. The throat chokes. O she was
insatiable candor in a vase too frail
of alabaster, that held an occult grail.
She evolved her prophesies as a seeress does.
Emaciated oracle of a word
uttered in an undegenerate tongue,
vernacular of universes young,
wild honey fed her, and the unwithering gourd
of the baptist crying in the wilderness,
in the desert, "Make straight the highway !" A voice said Cry
and, in her agony, with her dark burning eye,
her voice rang like a bird's, her amazing word
consumed our vanities. "Hath it not been told
you from the beginning !" And the echo rolled,
"Have ye not known, O nations ? Have ye not heard ?"

VASHTI

The heart of the king was merry with wine
    Bewraying his royal mien.
He called to his eunuch chamberlains
    To bring to him the queen.

Before the golden hammam screen,
    Silk-robed the eunuchs bowed.
Vashti the beautiful, the queen,
    Was opal in a cloud.

Her tiring-women thronged her round.
    The chamberlains bowed low.
Jewels were in the king's command,
    And yet she would not go.

The brow of the king was thunder black.
    His look flashed like the levin.
The Mede and Persian counsellors
    Before his throne were seven.

Tarshish, Carshena and Shethar,
    High lords in blood and breath;
Meres, Memucan, Marsena,
    Admatha — proud as death.

Of conquering Cyrus' royal seed
    The king did these inspire,
Even as Ormuzd rules each deed
    Through the altars of his Fire.

The Magians in their spell-wrought robes
    Heard the king's question come.
"What fate for this rebellious queen ?"
    It roared like a beaten drum.

Memucan spake and answered then
    How obduracy breeds.
"Let a new law stand in the laws
    Of the Persians and the Medes;

"An iron, unalterable law
    That wives their lords obey !"
Letters to all the satrapies
    Rode forth that selfsame day.

The great king's servants sought for him
    Virgins like grapes on vine.
But Vashti 'twixt the lions stood
    Like a chalice of gold wine.

Queen Vashti, like an Elburz moon,
    With wonderful dark eyes,
Took to proud breasts the shock of doom,
    And pondered on this wise:

"Mine empire and mine honours fall.
    Yet women shall be free.
I fairest was of women all
    And the king would boast of me.

"I come no more before the king
    As a slave after hire;
A bright chattel, a bought thing
    To move men's desire.

"Long may it be as it hath been,
        And womankind still bend;
Yet am I Vashti and the Queen
        Till this dark world shall end."

In Shushan, in the palace hall,
        Ahasuerus groaned.
Demoniac shadows on the wall
        Taunted his power enthroned.

The Angra Mainyu, Ahriman,
        With all his Daevas dire,
Darkened Ahura Mazda's light
        And railed against his Fire.

The haggard monarch's eyes confessed
        His loss and heavy dole,
For throat and brow, for limbs and breast,
        And the light in Vashti's soul.

THE LIGHT IN THE TEMPLE

Into the temple the gaunt old saint strode, by the Spirit led.
There a man, and a woman, and a small child sacrificed.
There, between seven-branched candlesticks, two dead wood-pigeons
bled;
But Simeon saw the Christ.

For the child turned on Simeon that dark gaze that charms and alarms,
And Israel's soul was stricken with a pang like the pain of the sword,
And Simeon's spirit quickened, and he lifted the child in his arms;
He lifted up Christ the Lord.

Hoarsely he cried, "O now Thou lettest thy servant depart in peace.
I have walked through dragon fires of darkness wherein thy world is
snared;
Yet, before the face of all, this hour, I have seen what doth not cease:
In the child, salvation prepared;

A light to lighten the Gentiles; Thine own people Israel's glory !"
. . Nearly two thousand years ago were those words by the prophet
said.
Now, in the day of apocalypse, we ponder the troubled story.
Our heaven quakes overhead.

Simeon blessed them, and said unto Mary the mother, "Behold this
child.
He is set for the fall and rising again of many in Israel.
And a sword shall pierce through thine own heart, from him, the small
and mild —
And the heart of Mankind as well."

Dark with famine lies half the world; in the core of life is danger;
With expectation the people cry and clamor on every hand.
And even once more, through blowing snow, there comes to Mankind
    a stranger;
        The Stranger, through every land.

For a moment stand with the prophet then, when the simple truth was
    gravèd
Deep in his soul; when mightier wings no chaos can destroy
Lightened on high; and there came to men, in the ancient city of David
        Good tidings of great joy.

ON A DEAD POET

For all they minimize and abrade away,
For all they say and say and still mis-say,
The living bronze has age on age for heirs.
What the detractors have is only theirs.

IV

THE FIRE IN THE CRYSTAL

THE FIRE IN THE CRYSTAL

*"The surface of the planet Earth seems to be a place for
the breeding and incarnation of souls."*

GUSTAF STRÖMBERG

That summer the shadow of war lay on his mind
who had driven far, and sat by candlelight
under the hand-hewn beams of the old inn
made quaint for travellers. The place was called
The Lobsterpot, happily only that
and not some ghastly punning name. The steak
sizzled in pewter on checked table-cloth.
He ate with relish, and with rumination
upon his pilgrimage. For it was hardly
that she, the poet whom he sought, had been
incomparable. She had been a woman
aromatic of the essence of the best
of a forgotten time, and had engrossed
the meditations, in a Midwest college
of this tall gaunt instructor, while her story
seemed, in an episode of later years,
somewhat of an enigma. So he was
in Northam, an antique New England village
by Kittiwake Cove, whither he'd steered his car
away from four-lane highways, wearying
of Coca-Cola, Esso, and Tydol signs
and U. S. 1, taking a winding sideroad
till he had reached the shore. He had the summer.
He had his notes and plans. He had his card
of registration that avowed his age
exempt from draft. He had this redbrown marvel
diminishing slowly on the plate before him

93

with the french fried potatoes and the beans
ambrosia on his tongue.
                                Thad Janeway looked
half railsplitter and half ambassador,
with thick dark hair that fell into his eyes,
and rawboned frame that yet was knit to grace.
A wisp curled bluely from his cigarette.
He thought of Copleys and of blue Dutch tile,
of Grinling Gibbons and Samuel McIntire;
He thought of punch-bowl ghosts and Cotton Mather,
of white coifed witches sorcerizing pigs
and making haycocks hang on trees. He saw
the blue sea twilight in the open window
above the rambler roses, and outside,
the golden rocks, and, clean on the expanse
of silken ocean, the notable Three Islands —
and, out beyond, the prison-house and shambles
of Europe at the mercy of a madman.
He thought of that. But in the haunted twilight
his thoughts were chiefly of Miranda Vail. . . .

She was a child of horizons. She had been
born on a lonely rock upon the sea.
Rasp of an infant crying in the dark
in a thick-walled stone cottage. A covered walk,
connecting with it, bridged a deep foamy chasm
to a lighthouse high and lone, that like a giant
loomed with black morion, and swung aloft
in the mirk evening air the lamps of crimson
and gold; an Atlas rooted in the rock
under the glitter of frosty winter stars. . . .

The child of five, curled on a window-seat
in the thickness of the wall, was the familiar

of lightning's crookèd swords, of wind and thunder
and surf unceasing, all the elements
besieging what she knew as home. She harkened
her elders drone of fabulous Santa Anna,
the war in Mexico, and Zachary Taylor,
in curtained lamplight; but ever through her brain
beat a dark tide, and ever, over all,
came cries through roaring of a battering sea,
as when in one fierce equinoctial gale —
tan-toaster, the fishers called it — as she watched,
from strangely coppercolored evening cloud
swooped headlong hurricane, and in the livid
and ghostly cannonade upon the rocks
a schooner, dragging anchor, crashed to doom
crushed like a colored cockle by the spuming
gigantic waves
               'Twas then a doryman
off from Shag Island, like a dried autumn leaf,
was whirled and carried along the coast of Maine.

The child-face at the chill wet window-glass,
wide-eyed and gasping, as the schooner *Fairhope*
with masts and yards like antlers of a stag,
and plunging like a stag, and lifting high
out of the wave, tore with a terrible rending
upon invisible rocks below; the *Fairhope*
that ever after through her dreams would drift
with eerie distant wailing of the doomed
lost dorymen.
               Her life had known three islands,
Kittiwake, Shag, and Scoldenore — for seafowl
named, and, perhaps, in landfall long ago
sighted by Captain Smith who built the cairn
on Appledore in Maine; named in the year

he may have named the promont of Cape Ann
Tragabigzanda for some Orient princess
of an Eastern venture. Bearded Captain Smith
south from Penobscot Bay, to the upcurled hook
white with the dunes on which the Pilgrims beached,
had surveyed all that coast. And yet the birds
named the Three Islands, the seafowl kin and kith:
kittiwake, froth or cloud; and cormorants
with black snake necks; and white-capped scoldenores;
the grebe, the coot, the gannet, the merganser;
for what is history or what is man
to the winged ones of the foam ? The barren rock,
the creviced rock of Kittiwake, whereon
the lighthouse stood, might stream with timeless seas;
while far ashore, beyond that barren outpost,
peace and plenty, the white cloud on the hill,
the coulter in the glebe, in sun-drowse shone —
or all the dark-piled thunderheads inhuman
of war reddened the sun — but in their season
still the wild duck and hungry mackerel gulls
were clamorous for food; still through the summer
the seabirds followed on the fishing hulls,
a shaken ribbon of rippled and veering wings,
with shrill discordant cries, who lived the law
of their own preservation, greed, and fury,
in converse to their moulded beauty of flight. . . .

Scoldenore cries in time of storm, they say,
as Appledore of the Isles of Shoals laments;
and it is haunted, like the bare rocks and bights
of Smutty Nose where once pale eyeless murder
walked with wild nightmare for a night and day —
although by no such horror — and Kittiwake
has superstitions too.

                    Upon the rock
of Kittiwake Light a little child grew older
to girlhood, through the phases of the moon,
the rhythm of seasons, change of sea and heaven:
a poet in the body of a woman
endowed with beauty and intrepidity,
and *anima divina* like a crystal
in *penetralia mentis.*
                              "Kittiwake Light !"
thought Janeway, dreamily, his Kansas fields
many leagues away. He rasped his chair
backward, and paid his bill, and left the inn,
and stood a moment under the evening sky
before the light inside an open store
revealing smudgy headlines that proclaimed
"Nazi Spearheads Seek Moscow," and again,
"Thunder Upon Two Fronts," while village youth
absorbed their "cokes." A shadow seemed to breathe
over him at the moment, an emanation
from more than any monster of the sea:
the shadow that was tyranny and terror,
the spirit choked and gagged in loathsome bonds,
the spread of evil from an ancient Europe.
Aware of shadow, he could also hear
real in his ears, an echo of heavy pulses,
a rhythmic pounding sound that seemed to grow
as the wind changed. It came abruptly now.
"Northam Tool Company !" a native said
upon the narrow walk. "She's loud tonight."
"Stamping out airplane parts for Uncle Sam;
sometimes you hardly hear it," said another.
"The red drop-forges are beside the road,
that make the racket, and the iron shutters
rolled up and open to give the boys a breeze !"

Janeway turned down the street and climbed a stoop
and mounted a dusty, dark and musty stair
to his temporary room. He stood awhile
at the open window, breathing in the sea.
He did not light the light. He watched the moon;
then sat upon the bed. . . .
                              It had begun
so long ago ! Perhaps it was because
he had been born far inland, and in fact
had never seen the eastern sea till now,
but always strangely in his soul had been
a lover of islands; and what was in her soul
was wrought by islands. There you touched the circle
of human limitation, for you lived
with the horizon. Yet in her life and friends
and eager heart, she had made it constantly
a circle that expanded. Poems and letters
of hers had shown him that; biographies
and dusty commentary. Homely verse
some fool had called her work. Not great, indeed,
not even first rate, perhaps; but with a light
upon her lines. He thought, why, even stumbling
dry furrows of a hot rustling Kansas cornfield
far inland, as a boy, he had known measure
of distance, and that lonely island light,
in his own soul.
                    She had robustly said,
with eyes upon the infinite horizon,
"I believe nothing, but I hope all things !"
And, as a little girl on Kittiwake,
it might have been a Prospero's own island,
such magic there she found. Of artless beauty
were her descriptions of the barren rock
endless in its enchantments: golden green

98

moss on bared ledges; Indian arrow-heads
of jasper in the little coves; striped snail
and mussel varnished blue; the tragic rusty
and ravelled ropeyarn of a driftwood spar;
the crimson calyx of a shadbush flower;
dulse, with a tang on the tongue; green-spined sea-urchins;
a lobster's mottled eggs; rosy herb-robert
among the rocks, and sea-anemones;
and through the soft air of a summer evening
the weird huge sigh that was a porpoise blowing;
torch of October in the huckleberries;
the streaks of purple tiderip in the twilight
upon a violet sea. Miranda knew
the sheeted rains of fall, the high gales tearing
fore-to'-gallant from boltrope, and in winter
some lumber schooner trudging a blurred coast
past the ice-girdled islands. She had witnessed
in northern heavens incredible coruscation
of the aurora; in the ocean spring
had felt the searing of bitter northwest wind,
and yet discovered in a rocky cranny
the bright stain of the anemone. It seemed
like her youth's inner radiance, of a nature
defeating dull monotony's metronome
and endless buffeting of the loud northwest
for twenty weeks till Spring.
                              Miranda learned
to turn her boat on its heel, to run it up
into the wind, to luff and come about
and lean on the other tack. She learned to sail
The Islands in a fog, by ear, as though
by the hard-bitten ghosts of coasters guided
who manned the picaroons. Yet she could write
later, still islanded, "I cannot tell you

how I dread the cold," and speak of wintry wind
"snowing and blowing like forty thousand devils!" . . .
"Black howling water in the brassy moonlight,"
she wrote again, who knew the wreck of schooners
and the drowned captains.
                              Yet her spirit was
the sea's for haleness, beauty, even for wildness
that shook her soul, and (read between the lines)
as trees uprooted by the hurricane
reveal the springs through which their roots are nourished,
so some rebellious passage in her journals
in poem or prose, some tense elliptical
tumultuous expression, had convinced
the western scholar that, through her life, there grew
vehemence which begot in later years
profound emotional storm, the time and place
and loved one coinciding.
                              He desired
to see what she had seen, as child and woman
of lonely ocean; to know what she had known;
the unknown quantity of her existence
to seek and find, could it indeed be found —
and not for vulgar curiosity,
but to complete the portrait of a soul
for all its vital data incomplete,
since there was mystery too. . . .

                              Below the wide
piazza steps of the antique hotel
he stood, still smelling metal, bilge, and varnish
of the small island steamer. Here it was.
The sign read "Guests." The rates were on the sign
tacked to a rain-stained plank on two cracked posts.
He thought how she had written one January

of the long piazza drifted deep with snow
from end to end, traversed by cows and sheep
where once romance and youth beneath the moon
lingered with thrills and whispering. And now
the men's Dundrearies, the French Empress bonnets,
the fans and furbelows were long since gone,
and the piazza boards were cracked and seamed. . . .
Then the screen creaked. A tall gaunt apparition,
an ancient, stood there staring, with one hand
rubbing his scanty beard. "Ye want — ?" he quavered.
Shades of the Concord writers who had graced
the halls within ! Was this indeed the hostel
in later years built by Miranda's father
when he resigned the light ? Its fame had grown,
and it had proved a hospice and a refuge
for artists and musicians — for the writer
and scholar — in those days before there bourgeoned,
all up and down the coast, that prodigy
American, the large summer hotel !
In, the East Parlor had not Miranda Vail
held an American salon, gathered round her
the talents of her time ?

                  The lobby breathed
a dank and musty odor of decay.
The desk revealed the open register,
impossible pen and ink, a rack behind
of many pigeonholes, and underfoot
he felt straw matting. Janeway pushed aside
a dog-eared Testament of greasy leather
and turned the register around, and signed.
He stood and noted that across the foyer
a broad stair mounted, and on either side
opened Victorian, high-ceilinged rooms.
"That the East Parlor ?" he asked. The apparition

said "Nup," and, several seconds later, added
"Through there. The wing." He fumbled from a hook
brass keys, and offered, "These here'll likely suit yeh."
"Meals ?"
                    "The sign says, don't it ?"
                                        Now they climbed,
stubbing upstairs against the old brass treads,
ancient ahead; a creaking corridor,
a sticky door forced open, and, "In here !"
Cracked window-shades askew and worn lace curtains,
complaining sashes, a dresser and a rocker,
a faded carpet, a big double bed;
even a fireplace, dark as Erebus.
"Bath's down the hall !" The bed had dubious springs
and lumps. That old mahogany chest-of-drawers,
however — but its larger upper part,
with the curled maple pillars, had no key.
"Nice," Janeway said. "How do you get this drawer — ?"
"Dunt," said the ancient. "Brung it daowun f'm th' attic.
Ben thar too long. Open them other drores !"
"I'll take the room," said Thad, "and what's your name ?"
"Bussard."
              "O ! . . . And how many guests are here ?"
"You're all."
              "So ? Many island visitors ?"
"Skurcely."
              Thad turned away. The ancient seized
his own large nose with one huge mottled paw
as though to wring it. His collarband and stud
moved to his adam's-apple. His cold blue eyes
hid in a mesh of wrinkles. His hair was gray
and tousled, and his faded overall
hung on a bony frame. Said Thad, "I'd like

to see the East Parlor. I've read so much about it."
The taciturn old turkey led him down.

Gloom, haircloth furniture, a corner cupboard
with old blue china; on the mantlepiece
sea-shells and minerals; a cabinet
of curiosities; things under glass;
white stones painted with oils; and one dark portrait
set in a frame of tarnished white-flaked gilt
flanked by two Biblical large steel engravings.
Framed photographs upon a drop-leaf table;
the shiny surface of the prints were yellowed,
Basques and bustles adorned the seated ladies;
the gentlemen had beards, high-buttoned coats,
tight trousers, and the ladies looped-up skirts
and balmorals; a casual striped blazer,
a waterfall chignon netted in chenille;
groups on porch-steps or grass, the attitudes
accentuated by the early camera.
And, among these, Miranda ?
                                    The room was long;
the faded window hangings all but hiding
the brilliant sea outside, across the ruin
of what must surely once have been her garden.
Could the room have been a blue delphinium bower,
with poppies red and yellow, phlox white and pink ?
Could she have sat on that black haircloth sofa,
Her eyes of cornflower blue, her silvered hair,
and the winged Mercury in intaglio
upon her breast ? Beneath that hideous lamp
could she have quietly read her poetry
with the french windows of the parlor open
to ocean moonlight, and around the room

naturalist and poet, opera singer,
'cellist or painter ?

              "It can't be as she had it !"

"Mis' Vail, yeh mean ? Her fambly tuk her things
long time ago. A few stored in the attic,
mostly all gone."

             "Did you know Mrs. Vail ?"

"Nup. Never. 'Fore my time."

                  Not, Janeway guessed,
by many years. "Her cottage was beyond
that — garden ?"

             "Yup. Still see the cellar-hole."

Janeway walked to the window, stood and stared,
then turned. " Someone, perhaps, can row me over
to Kittiwake some day ?"

             "Luke."

                  "Good enough."

Lying awake among the strange contours
of the bed's mattress, through the open window
light followed night as the far lighthouse flashed.
Some of Luke's phrases from the day just done
"flittered like pickerel" within his mind,
though in the language Luke had then applied
to the house-cat, Thaddeus upon his quest
had proved "no great of a mouser." What was that
about the "haddick" slipping through "Old Horny's"
fingers, "leavin' that black stripe" ? Stocky Luke
was a weather-toughened lad of fifteen years
burned to a mottled tint; red nose and wrists,

puzzled brown freckled face. And he was ruled
by Bussard with an iron rod. A female
named Beulah did the beds and got the meals
decent though unadorned. Thad had acquired
from Bussard (christened Lemuel, he found)
a large work-table where were spread his papers
and notebooks and biographies. He saw it
looming across the room, and through the window
noted that (Luke's expression) "a growin' moon
chaws up the clouds !"

His trip to Kittiwake
had made Miranda more vivid than before.
He saw a shy girl with a roseleaf face
and the figure of a nymph, and overflowing
laughter, a sea-sprite in a poplin dress
with a mermaiden glance, and tinted shells
at neck and wrists.

She was but seventeen
when Daniel Vail rowed her from Kittiwake
to Scoldenore, and lifted her across
the threshold of a minister's abode
since to the reckless island fisherfolk
he had come to be lay preacher. Tall and dark
student and lawyer was this Daniel Vail,
graduate of Harvard, with religious zeal
in judgment come to red-baize-shirted exiles
fallen on dissolute and degraded days.
But, more and more, piety grew upon him
until the color and the early burnish
ideas took in his mind were tarnished over
with bigotry and dogma, and he went
a man possessed by a dark dream of God
impressive to the superstitious folk
but by Miranda, in their intimate life,

known as close to mania. She was daughter
of a father heretic and independent,
a man of lineage and great energy,
a strong rebellious soul who early left
life on the mainland, to tend a lonely light,
spurning the mundane bicker; his wife, her mother,
the husband's loyal shadow.
                                        It was there,
on Scoldenore, Miranda wrote her poem
elaborated from the actual
death of a glorious bird on Kittiwake
beating its life out against the lighthouse glass.
She called it merely "The Eagle and the Lantern,"
a parable of the soul.
                              On Kittiwake
Janeway had seen the new and modern light
which superseded older edifice.
The cluster of five red reflector lamps
and ten of gold, of old, had given place
now to a many-prismed Fresnel lens.
But still the stanchioned covered walk, across
the narrow chasm, was as Miranda knew it
From the house where she was born.
                                        The boat had floated
in at the end of a long mossy slip
below the boathouse. The assistant keeper,
named Allen, helped him up the narrow treads
beside the skids, and the first boat he saw
in the boathouse showed him by its lettering
the Coast Guard was in charge. He saw before him
a storehouse painted red, and two white houses
with red foundations; and behind them rose,
small-windowed, the white housing of the walk
aslant to the tall white tower of the Light,

flanked by the fog-horn structure. Janeway stepped
to the fissure spanned, and found it at this tide
dry and undangerous. So calm the sea
around the little island, who could image
those giant gales ? There was no sound, it seemed
more than the gentle rustling of the swell
in sunlit peace. In the lightkeeper's house
they crossed the modern kitchen, where his wife
excused herself to clear the mid-day meal.
In the living-room Thad could imagine clearly
pot-hooks and trammels on a swinging crane
in the dark fireplace, and a coffee-pot
set on a trivet, as it once had been.
The deep-set windows and original walls
still stood. Beyond the fireplace, a door
led to the covered walk. Payne, the lightkeeper,
said in a pleasant drawl, "This here old stone
was built to stay. We overhauled the chimney
some years ago. We still got timbers here
of the original house, though all the floor
is new. Look here !" he strode across the room
and turned the knob. The door showed open air.
"The way up to the tower. Wanta see ?"
They stepped a yard of ground. Another door
was opened, and they walked on an incline
of darkly painted floor, a narrow way.
Ladders, a fire-extinguisher, regulations
hung on the walls. There was a book to sign;
small windows set at intervals; the roof
not high above the head. He saw and passed
two stationary engines. Then his foot
was on a special iron fretwork stair
with a rope rail. They climbed, as Payne explained
how he replenished the tank of kerosene

and kept the air tank always "eighty pressure."
And Janeway recollected how Miranda
had called the winter cottage "a Bastille"
and, like a prisoner, had tended plants
in window niches: rose-geraniums,
pinks, and oxalis.
           Up in the lantern now,
to gape at glittering bullseyes, and the facets
of the great lens; to listen to Payne explaining
the clockwork that revolved the giant eye.
But standing steeply on the iron step
to hark the keeper on holophotal prisms
and peer inside the lens, and have him tell
about the vaporizer and the mantel,
Thad managed, at last, to venture out upon
the narrow outside gallery. Above
the island he stood, above the peacock sea,
remembering that Miranda had declared
the white gulls gathered up the golden sunshine
in the arch of their snowy wings.
              And then again
Payne was telling, as they were going down,
of the fog signal's patent air-compresser
and how in every twenty-seven seconds
the horn blasted for three, and how the lamp
was fifty-five millimeter; till they stood
in the whitewashed room again, and there were thanks,
goodbyes, and come-agains. . . .
              Full of the day,
he lay awake upon his lumpy mattress
in the balmy summer night. And now at last
he thought of Avery Sutton — Avery Sutton,
Miranda's friend, the artist Avery
recurring in her journals, the eminent

marine painter who came to take a room
in this hotel so famous in the islands
built by Miranda's father, where the family
had one whole wing. For partly Avery's story
it was that drew him from his western college.
So he rose now, switched on the lamp, and read
for the twentieth time:
                              "Sutton's condition seemed
exhaustion from the work on certain murals,
a commission occupying many months,
the difficult painting always manifesting
a tendency to sink into the stone;
the deadline for the scaffolding's removal
weighing the artist's conscience. Prior to this
his wife died suddenly, after many years
of married life."
                              A theory of Thad's
was of a rapidly deepening intimacy
between Miranda and the haggard artist
during his island sojourn. Said the book:
"One morning, missing at breakfast, Sutton seemed
completely to have vanished. Through the day
they searched. Then, in a deep ravine of traprock
at the island's end, the body of the drowned
was found by Mrs. Vail. The episode
shadowed her mind for years."
                              A widowed grief,
mixed with his overwork and overstrain ?
And if the poised and gracious island hostess
had sought to bring him comfort, was it strange ?
What sadness, knowing that her help had failed !
Or was it merely that ? Or was he tricked
by a dramatic reading of the past ?
The later Mrs. Vail at middle age

Had still the fresh complexion of her youth
and the enthusiasm of those years
mellowed by kindness and by understanding;
and though so busied in her island garden
with weeding and transplanting — recommender
of clayey soil for zinnias, commentator
on the useful garden toad — in her there lived
the ardent, tender girl of Kittiwake,
the elfin of horizons, child of tumult
and infinite languor of the summer sea,
with whom an impassioned theist of the time,
her preaching Daniel, wrestling vigorously
for God on Scoldenore, tall, thin, and dark
with burning eyes — and worshipping his wife —
begot three sturdy children, while in gusts
of other passion he exhorted her
to save her soul, she who was free and stalwart
as the sea air and granite; even in
rebellions of her youth, a staunchly loyal
woman of love and laughter !
                                   Had the years
like waves upon the rock that was her faith,
within her doubts, worn down the causeway bridging
the chasm between two natures ? As a girl
it had fascinated Vail to train her spirit,
serving as guide and mentor; till there flowered
her natural and unaffected gift
for simple verse. Then suddenly her thought
broke through the strictness of his admonitions,
in poetry, and blinded by the light
of God — the eagle buffeting at the glass —
strove in strong rhythms. And when at last there came,
albeit worn and frail, the subtler mind
which seemed for a miraculous interval

the complement of hers — ?

There were her words
in a known letter, "The painter Leonardo
may really have looked like that !"

Years ere they met,
the preaching Daniel had left Scoldenore
to travel through the land upon a "sending,"
a visitation; and as he followed God,
he left Miranda with her widowed mother
to superintend the caravansery
in summer on Shag Island, spend the winters
close-exiled there ! till finally his letters
failed, and he disappeared beyond the reach
of all inquiry, leaving her with children
grown and dispersed; and whether, in her forties,
bereft of husband or not, she never knew
and none could ascertain. . . .

So Janeway drifted
to sleep — and woke to song-sparrows in the trees.

Down in the lobby, and behind the desk,
Bussard slumped in a chair with leather cushion
gone at the seams. With spectacles on nose
he thumbed his greasy Bible.

Janeway said,
" 'Morning !" and was for passing. But no answer,
save for a nasal mumbling, came from Lemuel,
and Thad discovered the boniface pronouncing,
albeit in accents blurred, "And Abraham
said unto his young men — ." He started then
and noticed Janeway, and his chair came down
on its front legs, and one gnarled hand went up
and stroked his forehead. But he did not speak.

So Thad passed, calling, "Luke !"

        "Daown t' th' float !"

a voice hallooed.

    Thad stood within the door
of the lightkeeper's cottage, in late morning,
the hot sun high. He knocked upon the panel,
then faced an empty kitchen, paused, and crossed
to the far chamber with the dark old fireplace,
flowers in the window-niches, and the door
to the lighthouse passageway. It stood half open.
He called, "Hello there !" No one. He remembered,
as Luke had not, today the lighthouse keeper
and wife were for the mainland. The assistant
must be somewhere around. Thad glanced about.
The room was filled with sun. He almost thought
it also held a presence. A quick step
and Allen stood in the half-opened door
from the passageway. "Hello !" was all he said.
"Hello !" said Thad. "You know I clean forgot
the Paynes had gone to Northam for the day !"
"That's right. But never mind. Had any lunch ?
I came in for a bit myself. Suh busy
paintin' up there, an' polishin' !" They ate
together, and Allen, saying, "Well, I'll see yeh !"
was gone as he had come.

       The room was silent
and full of summer sun. The thick white walls
with their deep window-niches, low white ceiling,
incongruous mail-order furniture,
the radio and the wall telephone . . .
the nets of sunlight . . . golden . . . shining peace. . . .
A cloud had stolen over the island, shadow
had entered . . . darkness. . . . Janeway heard the birds

blundering in darkness at the great high lantern
as souls must blunder against the light of God
glassed from them by complete inapprehension. . . .
And that May morning she had told him of
when at the foot of the tower rock she found
the limp small bodies of sparrow, swallow, thrush,
and purple finch and golden oriole,
and gathered them within her pinafore . . .
and once two gulls had cracked a large clear pane,
and the fire-winged and many-colored warbler
had splintered beak, a bird all life and song
lost in the sea-mist. . . .

                 How the mid-day heat
drowsed in the house ! He found that he was lying
in a window embrasure. He hardly knew
when he had there reclined. He wadded up
his coat for a pillow. . . .

                 There was a little sound
that brought him to one elbow, all befogged
it seemed, by sleep. The door beyond the fireplace
that gave upon the entrance to the lighthouse
was open, but on darkness, save for mist
of faintest light. There stood a little girl.
And yet there was no such upon the island.
The Paynes were childless. Shy but resolute,
and holding to her breast a wounded bird,
she moved without a sound into the room;
and by what light he saw her now he did not
precisely know. Yet he was sure he heard
her tiny voice say clearly to him, "*Fly
in the hollow of the wave !*" Then she looked down
upon the faintly fluttering bird. He found
his lips frame, "Why ?" The small and lovely voice
said very clearly now inside his head,

"Because that way the petrels fly through storm,
in the hollow of the wave."
                              It seemed to him
he dared not breathe. She said, "The bird was wounded
beating against the Light. It is too great —
the Light. They do not know." He held his breath.
She said, "And I was wounded by the light."
It seemed her eyes were living in his soul
with pain and ecstasy . . . and in the room
the sunlight was a glory; there it lay
patterned upon the floor . . . and where she was
she was not. Of the covered way the door
was closed. He stood. His feet were manacled
with dream. . . . He heard the voices from the landing
of the lightkeeper and wife. . . .

                              The swishing oars
rattled in their rowlocks, as Luke bent his back.
"Little soul . . . a cloud, a feather . . ." murmured Janeway
remembering a modern poet's version
of Hadrian's Address, and, "Do you play
as before . . . ?" He shrugged his shoulders and shook off
bewilderment, and said to Luke, "Your father's
quite a Bible reader."
                    "Father ?"
                              " Mr. Bussard."
"He ain't my father !"
                    "Oh !"
                              "Though he's religious
as all git out. They say he tuk a shock
when his wife died. Allus ben quare sence then.
He — "
          "Well, go on !"

                    "Vally my job I do."
"You can trust me."
                "Aw, nawthin' much."
                        A silence.
Then Luke, as though he were really only talking
to himself, *sotto voce*, "O, I reckon
it's what the most men do — that Sarah Stebbins.
They run her out of town. 'Twas then he got
religion hard. And now he'll up an' roar
at me of all the devils in the flesh."
He spat. "I talk t' much." And he resumed
his swing upon the oars.

                    Within the room
that evening, by the lamp, "It was," read Thad,
"approximately at this time that she
discovered in herself mesmeric power,
as she believed. I had the great good fortune,"
the rather dull biographer went on,
"to be present at one seance at the house
of a friend in Northam, when it was reported
messages were conveyed to various persons
in the room, from the other world. We know that she
believed in spiritism, and became,
though temporarily, a follower
of the Theosophists. But then her mind
asserted itself again, and she decided
that commerce with the supernatural
was undermining both her health and spirits.
In later years she rarely would indulge
such weakness. Yet I well recall one evening
in her father's hostelry upon Shag Island
when the planchette was produced. . . ."

115

Validity
of clairvoyance ? But thoughts can be transferred. . . .
Varius on Memory. He was at Western.
He claimed we do not realise our powers
of apperception and of memory.
We don't know how the memories in the brain
operate, or how cosmic radiation
may act. I've heard him say he didn't think
whatever organizes memory
is modified by death. . . .
                        Thad Janeway rose
and stood beside the window, and the sea
out in the dark, drew a long suspiration
that sounded like a human sigh, as though,
" as though," it said, "as though we two were fated,
from the first seeing. . . ."
                        Janeway frowned, and turned,
and paced the lamplight. . . . Was it Strömberg said
"The memory of the individual
is written in indelible script upon
both space and time" ? I can't forget that line !
There's a whole train of reasoning. But Varius
accepts telepathy, materialization,
one person to another, without limit
of space or time. It may be apparition
of those but lately dead or those who died
long years ago. Appearance may take place
where the momentous has occurred, or else
actuated by other circumstance.
There's Strömberg's story of the hidden temple
in a jungle in Ceylon. Two travelling
English photographers saw a Hindu girl
dancing in sunlight on the temple steps.
So one set up his camera, and viewed

the dancer in the finder, cranked the camera —
and suddenly the girl had disappeared.
The developed film showed nothing. Yet his friend
corroborated everything. Well, Varius
of course says individual memories
persist even after death, events connected
with intense emotion can be activated. . . .
His thought trailed off, though scraps from Crookes and Wallace,
Flammarion and Lombroso, floated on
the surface of a mind that never was
a mechanist's. He thought: suppose a child,
even a child, in piercing childish sorrow
at finding a dead bird, a wounded bird —
some childhood memories endure a lifetime —
and why not after death ? The ghost by noonday:
evocation, emanation. . . .
                                        At the window
now he could see, from Kittiwake nearby,
a bright shaft sweep, followed by one of shadow,
across a point of rock, and finger far
out into ocean. The arms of light revolved
as every night he had perceived them shine,
accepted like a planetary motion.
The path lingered and darkened on the sea,
on wide mysterious ocean, where somewhere
out there, beneath the horizon, there arose
the strange "foam-fountain of the mighty whale."
And as the seeking beam of searchlight circled,
he thought, how all things lead me back to her
who craves release. And why did I think that
he thought a second later ? *Who craves release ?*
As for the living soul, did she not say,
"Did you ever watch the fading of a life
and how the dying pass from behind their eyes

precisely as a face looks from a window
and then is gone ? Extinguished ? O, but never !
Simply a passing from behind the window
from which we have looked out for all our lives."
Remembering this, he now prepared for rest,
losing the searchlight beams from where he lay.
He thought, her presence is all about these islands.
She asks a boon of me . . . a resolution
of something . . . and he slept. . . .

                       The powder-blue
of the East was streaked with fiery rose, a bright
syllabling rippled like rills and bubbles of
some high aërial rivulet, from birds
just wakened. A film of curtain faintly stirred
in the dawn breeze. He found that he was standing
and slipping arms into his dressing-gown
and cording it. His feet were in his slippers.
And he was at the door, and in the hall,
and at the stairhead. One heel clicked against
a tread, brass-reinforced. He hurried down
and crossed the empty lobby and passed under
the arch, and came to the East Parlor doors.

Already the morning was brighter than he thought.
The room had changed completely. It was large
but light and airy, with scatter-rugs of green
upon a hardwood floor; and he could see
the windows open on the long piazza,
the unfamiliar paintings on the walls
above the shelves of books, and there beyond
across the room an ebony piano
of concert style, and glimmering everywhere,
indoors and out, flames of fresh garden flowers:

nasturtiums on the mantel, from pale yellow
to gleaming red; marigold, coreopsis,
chrysanthemum, on book-cases and tables;
among the couches with the colored pillows,
in sapphire or in red Bohemian glass,
the larkspur and sweet peas. Especially
a burgundy rose glowed in a tall green vase,
Gabrielle de Luizets in a celadon
green bowl; and rainbow shells, and water-lilies
in white-threaded gold-dusted Venice glass.
Past the tall open windows, viny green;
and, beyond that again, the hollyhocks
of white and pink and scarlet, sentinel
among the sunflowers. Over all this shimmer,
the bee and butterfly and humming-bird.
And everywhere, through all and over all,
the tissue flutter and the myriad tints
of those dream flowers, the poppies, whether yellow
Iceland, or white and shining as a bride,
or gorgeous scarlet. In their gray-green leaves,
in lucent glass, others were being carried
in from the garden, as, with draperies
floating, advanced the lady of the poppies
before whose bosom they blew in cloud and flame,
crimson or burning gold. The effluence
of poppy streamed invisibly about
the still, enchanted scene. Beyond the windows,
a sea of color under dagger-darts
of jewelled wings; and the bleached ledges leaned
toward brilliant ocean. . . .
                              Then the sunlit room
wavered, as though a prospect undersea
trembled from movement of the rippled water.
The ministering figure turned her head,

and everywhere, it seemed, there were disposed
in listening attitudes in the apartment
an audience, in quaintly-fashioned gowns
whispering like the petals of a dream,
faces as evanescent as the wing
of the sphinx moth, and shadowy men who murmured
their approbation of insistent music,
pervading music, that was mixed somehow
with a wild bird's sonata in the garden.
Then one of them moved forward. He was tall
and courtly, and bowed slightly to the lady
who held the poppies. To Janeway's inner ear
he said, "Beyond dark scripture, dear Miranda !
Color and light and joy — you are your flowers,
the flowers you love so much, for you are in them
and of them, wholly !" . . . and then wavering,
they all were wavering . . . and glimmering . . .
dissolving . . .

        Janeway knew that he was standing
shivering uncontrollably, alone
in the doorway of a bleak brown empty room
dark-draped and set with haircloth furniture
black and repellent, and with ugly pictures,
and things imprisoned under airless glass.
And then he heard the croak of Lemuel Bussard,
a creaking step behind him, and the words,
"Daown airly, Mister. I — "

        He stood again
inside his room, and now it came upon him
Miranda was "the most auspicious star"
of this strange island. Was Luke, transmogrified,
its Caliban — Lemuel counterpart
of the damned witch, Sycorax ? But then whose soul

raged in the cloven pine ? Not Ariel's
but his own spirit, darker, heavier,
caught in the toils of mystery. He groaned
at the conceit, in several senses. He
would go to Scoldenore!

                    Luke manfully
tugged at the oarlocks of the broad-beamed dory.
The cloudless day was opportune. Thad knew
on Scoldenore there now remained no trace
of meeting-house or parsonage or any
cots of the fishers. Since the obliteration
by wind-swept fire some twenty years ago,
it was all open to the elements
as a medrake's nest. In the surf's intermission
you might hear the eerie laughter of the loon,
that high clear shriek that ended in a shudder
of lonesome sound, as the bird oared the bights
about the island. A mad, dark island this.
He knew its legends. As a New England poet
had said, it was the illimitable sweep
of sky and water that greatly magnified
imagination. The fog in its own season
summoned the figures of mirage. The winds
of night spoke with strange voices. Lawless and wild
this one of the Three Islands, fitly named
for the *clangula hyemalis* — barren rocks,
predestined harborage of those who sailed
with letters of reprisal or of marque;
to the pirate, the seal-hunter, the runagate
and refugee, the broken cavaliers
who fled for hiding, after the Royal cause
went down in England. Here, in early days,
lounged the rough fisherman in Monmouth cap

and leathern jerkin and heavy scaly seaboots,
smoking Brazil tobacco, joking loudly
with raucous fishwives as they mended nets.
Plenty of pinnaces then, plenty of ketches
in harbor — flakes were spread with drying fish.
Ordinaries and ale-houses were doing
a driving business, till catspaws clawed the ocean
to breeze, and fishers bent sail to be gone
to north and east. Many a night of seafog
and gathering storm, the tavern windows blinked
as the company within tossed off rhum-bullion,
or passado, or Barbadoes. Over the roar
of the surf, the fo'castle shantey loudly rose,
with a Micmac Indian fiddling wild to clear
the tavern floor for bloods to shake it, whirling
their doxies in the brantle. . . .

                             Drawing near
the rocky shore, Luke figured his approach
to the old dock, a strip of sand and gravel
coarse, fish-bone-filled, lying beyond its jut.
Freebooters ? Were their swaggering ghosts alurk
above, on the Spanish graves — or later, weaker
early-Nineteenth-Century denizens
turned drunken and degraded, challenging
Heaven itself with their impieties,
stoning the parson and moderator from them,
spawning their white-faced and consumptive children,
women of dried-fish-color, puffing black
tobacco pipes, men sodden with rum, dull brutes ?
"Nasty-faced chowder-heads they was, they say !"
Luke offered, as he pulled one oar and pushed
the other, and hardly with a glance around
snugged to the dock. "I'll haul off now an' float

a cod-line, whilst ye walk about," he said.
Thad climbed and walked a string-piece. "Give a hail,"
said Luke, "when 'tis ye want me !"

                               Up went Thad
with a light step, through bushes and coarse grass.
The mackerel gulls rose screaming and soared away.
But good bright sun was hot upon his back.
He came upon a venerable fragment
of old stone wall, crawled by a golden lichen,
beset by thistles; and, just by chance, avoided
plumbing the hollow of an ancient cellar
scattered with brick and lime. His nostrils tingled
to bayberry and sweet fern. The crevices
of old irregular ruins sprouted weeds,
and down in ragged fissures by the shore
raspberry bushes clung, and pink wild rose
fluttered wet ground. He walked on rocks by chasms
where deep the tide-wash foamed. And then he rounded
a boulder, and was suddenly aware
of someone on the sky. A rough stone cairn
rose out of shin-deep scrub. It looked as though
the figure, bent up there against blue heaven,
were adding to it rocks. Now the man's head
turned in profile, and, with a thump of pulse,
the visage and the jaw of Lemuel
were plain to Janeway. The old man discoursed,
shoving an obdurate rock. His thin voice came
clear through the island stillness.

                               "I sojourned
in the Philistine's land . . . but 'Bimilech's servants
took off my well of water. . . . 'Bimilech
will make no covenant with me. . . ." It faded
to other unintelligible words.
What scriptural duty this ? To build a well-curb

on solid rock, where there was dug no well ?
But as Thad watched, the old man seemed to sense
a presence. He glanced around with deep suspicion
as Thad stepped quickly back behind the boulder.
He shuffled off, and swiftly disappeared
around a point of rock. Cautiously, slowly,
Thad neared the cairn. A mere agglomeration
of random stones, no more coherence to it
than had the words of its furtive and abortive
architect ! Thad explored on Scoldenore,
but did not chance again on Lemuel
till, at the mile-long island's farther end,
beneath him opened a rough brief beach, and there
beyond, a small boat with some sort of motor
cut a swift wake, seeming, in widening sweep,
to aim toward Shag.

As Thad retraced his steps
to rejoin and hail the patient fisher, Luke,
he knew he passed the site of ancient vice
and grimly waged religion; yet he felt,
here in the sun, somehow, a shining word
accompany him. An exquisite amethystine
humming-bird suddenly darted through the sunlight.
Limpid aquamarine in afternoon
the ocean rippled. It seemed indeed to him
a well-remembered voice breathed in his ear,
"Even here there was such beauty under heaven;
even here mankind befouled it; even here
they were taught of a dark God of punishment."
It thinned and died.

And soon Thad sat bemused
within the dory, watching flopping fish
on slimy floor-boards, hearing the bait-can rattle,
debating in his mind, and casually

asking, "Has Bussard got another boat ?"
"Yare. One with a kicker. But he wunt
let me to use it."

             No boat was at the landing.
It must be kept elsewhere. Crossing the lobby,
Lem sat behind the desk, grunted a greeting,
crouched to his Bible.

                   It was on that night
that Janeway dreamed. . . .

                        He stood within the tower
of Kittiwake Light. He saw the iron door
of the former iron lantern there above.
It seemed a windless evening near to sunset.
There was no breath of air to stir the flames
in the old reflector. Then he saw that something
in the lit dome, between the old-fashioned lamps,
seemed to vibrate: the delicate palegreen
of a Luna moth, its crescents and brown markings,
and like the long tail-feathers of a swallow
its frailer underwings. Exquisitely
it floated above him, like a wraith of moonlight;
and ever agitatedly it beat
like the inevitable psyche, whirling,
spiralling downward, around and round the flame. . . .

Into pale dawn he woke, and, leaning up
mazed in his vision still, he seemed to see
a diaphaneity of someone standing
before the window, nor could the little rustle
of leafage be the whisper of that voice,
"*Avery is walking in the rain,*"
it said, "*And Avery was in this room.*
Save Avery and me ! Now he is lying
caught in the rocks, washed over by the sea.

'No, never !' I said." (Weeping) *"I said 'No, never !'*
And you must find, and take from me, because
I said 'No, never !' against my leaping heart,
and saw his stricken eyes. But O what else
to his sudden rush of words was I to say
except the tolling words, 'O never, never !'
who saw love living, but knew not if love lived ?
Now you must find . . . but not because . . ." More weepi
strangled the thin and lost and urgent voice
heard as from far in the clairaudient hour
of dawn; but she was visible as she turned
though dimly only. Now her voice had changed,
rapid and low and earnest, *"It is dark*
on Scoldenore. We could not help the people.
He said at last we could not help the people.
It was dark in Daniel. It was dark in me.
And then the sun at last, after those years.
The sun so blinding — O the sun so late !"
And then she said, *"Too far into the mist.*
You are walking in deep mist. Avery walked
into the mist, though not into the dark
like Daniel. Yet there is a dark like Daniel's,
a shadow on Scoldenore. O now go quickly —
O go to Scoldenore !" And, as she was,
she was not there.

　　　　　　　The blisters on his palms
at least assured him of reality
as now they gripped and hauled the smooth oar-handles
of the dory, and his unaccustomed tendons
ached with his effort. The sea lay dead and calm
and Scoldenore was near. He clumsily
bumped at the dock, and made the dory fast,
and ran the path.

No mackerel gulls this time
rose to shriek out on him and veer away.
He passed by wall and cellar-hole and fissure,
skirted the traprock dyke; zigzagging clambered,
trod on the edge of chasms — a queer wild hurry
in his heart and in the thudding of his pulse;
and pushing out of spiny furze he rounded
the boulder still familiar. He looked upward
to see two figures sharply silhouetted
against the dawn. He saw that Luke laid down
a heavy load of driftwood and of brushwood
on the stony cairn. He heard his one word, "Thar!"
on a note of mutiny. The strange old man
raised up his hands, in menace or in prayer?
He said, "Be still! A beacon it is to be
beyond yer knowin'!"

                      "Why would yeh want a beacon?"
The voice of Luke was surly and afraid.
"Be still!" the old man said, "God hears. Kneel down!"
"Yer cra — !"

              "Kneel down!" said in a voice of thunder.
Luke stood with head bent, a refractory bullock.
"Kneel down," cried the old man, "Isaac!"

                          "I be — !"
"Ye be the son o' me an' Sarah Stebbins.
They tuk away from me my well o' water.
They druv my Sarah off. I prayed to God
for retribution agin' my false accusers.
I make my sacrifice to God. Kneel down!"
Silence. Then, far off in the clear still air,
the wild shriek and final shuddering chuckle
of the uncanny loon. The old man's voice
rose rasping hard, "An' wood fer the burnt offerin'!
Hold out yer hands!"

Luke's voice was stammering,
"Ye lie ! What air ye aimin' — ?"
But the knife
was gripped by the old man, as Luke's hands rose
caught like lightning within the other's grasp
and bound with cord.
"Why are ye tyin' me ?"

Then Thad shouted, who had been clambering close,
yet spoke not as the God of Abraham
but hurled himself on Bussard. Both went down,
and the knife was kicked away.
"What bloody nonsense !"
gasped Janeway. But the ancient now lay still
and a thin thread of blood was running from
his chin, where his pale lip was bitten through.
Panting, Thad felt his heart and, reassured,
untied Luke's bonds and tied the ancient's hands
with the same cord. Said Luke, "He's preachin' crazy !
He allus skeered the daylights outa me.
Some kind o' kin to me — but he was sayin'
he was my father ! He sez to me this mornin'
the Angel o' the Lord has spoken to 'm
an' he gotta build a beacon — an' I thought
the best was jest to humor him. I thought
mebbe he's goin' to signal to them Germans
we're fightin' in the War. I better see,
an' mebbe turn 'm in !"
"We'll take him back,"
said Janeway, "to the boat. Tie up his feet
now, with this other cord ! We'll get to Shag
and send for Payne."
They carried him, and found
the other boat, and got him in the "kicker"

towing the dory. He remained unconscious
till Beulah met them. At last his gawky length
was lifted into bed, and Beulah went
lamenting nasally, and brought hot water
and arnica; and the old man awoke
and babbled incoherently, and struggled
until they had to bind him to the bed.

So, at the last, the Paynes had come, and brought
a doctor from the mainland. They took over,
and Thad, upstairs, threw himself on his bed
and slept from sheer exhaustion. As he slept
it seemed he dreamed . . . it seemed that he was lying
in the lightkeeper's window embrasure
on Kittiwake, as he had lain that day
of haunted sunlight; and the door that led
to the tower opened, and the child figure stood
again against that strange square patch of darkness
between the house and covered walk, where always
there was light and open air. The child came slowly
into the room, and said, like ripply water,
and as though talking to another child,
"The kelps are very slippery and brown
and I have cut them into little men
and called them kelpies. They wither in the wind
and blow away. I make them sail on boats
of driftwood. I have fleets of musselshells
in pools among the rocks."

                          She seemed to hold
a small red flower. She said, "You know this is
the poor man's weather-glass — although," quite primly,
"some say the pimpernel." And then her forehead
puckered, "And a white flower," she said, "a new
white flower that blossoms overnight. . . ." She frowned

with effort of her thought. Thad heard himself
ask her, "Are you Miranda ?"
                          "She is mine.
She is a wilful child."
                          "A child ?" asked Thad
in the mazes of his dream.
                          "O yes ! My child.
She does not understand so well. You see
she first was me. But now I have come back."
If Thad said, "Why ?" it seemed a natural thing.
The child regarded him with grave blue eyes.
"There was a storm here once, the sea roared over
the rocks here; it roared under the covered walk,
and in the chasm. There was an awful noise.
The walk was torn away . . . there was a storm,
a storm . . . I cannot tell. . . ."
                          It seemed to him
that, at those words, a sudden roar of waters
rose in the room around them, and the child
was now a child no longer, but a woman
come to old age, with still a roseleaf face
and silvery hair. "A storm," she said, "a storm
O leaving me so shaken — leaving him — !"
Then strangely, out of Thad's own memory,
a tag of Latin, an old and hallowed phrase,
"Quoniam in aeternum misericordia Eius . . .
Who is mightier than the noise of many waters . . . !"

Janeway awoke to noise within the room
and found the shade was flapping at the window
since a strong wind had risen. The sky was dark
with evening. An impulsion in his mind
of something he must do . . . an inner voice

said to him there was something he must find. . . .
He left the bed and went to close the window.
It was as strong upon him as a hand
gripping his arm; and, standing in the room,
looking about him wildly, he was sure
she wished . . . and then he took a step, and stood
before the old mahogany chest-of-drawers
that would not open, relic of old days
brought down out of the attic. With his hands
he felt across its surface here and there,
fingered along the ornamental border,
and, in the floriate carven decoration,
his fingers were upon a knob that moved.
He turned it; drawing forth an upedged panel.
Its mate slid out upon the other side.
And now the entire front of the top drawer
moved outward, creaking down toward these supports,
held by a lower hinge. He helped it down,
and the desk stood revealed. The desk was covered
by motheaten green baize; and at the back
were pigeonholes. The small and square compartments
seemed empty, save for one, and out of this
Thad drew, at length, a pamphlet and a book.
His hands trembled a little as he laid them
upon the table. He sat down. He lifted
the pamphlet — an exhibition catalogue —
the sale "by public auction 1 P.M.
at Horticultural Hall," a sale of paintings
by the late Avery Sutton. There was also
a printed story of the artist's life
and, laid within, a yellowed photograph.
The face looked forth from it with haunting eyes
and fine patrician features. Thad examined

the text, noted the years at Harvard College,
the winters spent in Rome, the student days
at Düsseldorf and Barbizon, the visit
to Holland, the absorbed investigation
of the properties of light, travels in Spain
and the near East, marriage to Edith Travis
of Boston; titles of pictures here: "Charles River,"
"West Gloucester Beach," "The Rocks at Pigeon Cove."
Gently he put it down, and then took up
the book, an early American edition
of Ruskin's lectures, "Sesame and Lilies."
"Miranda from Avery" the flyleaf said,
and underneath, " — the highest, farthest flung;
the decuman wave —." He fingered at the book.
It opened easily to other pages,
the second of Ruskin's lectures, "Of Queens' Gardens."
In the translation of the ancient verses
of the Knight of Pisa to his living lady
this verse was underlined,

> "Lady, since I conceived
> Thy pleasurable aspect in my heart,
> My life has been apart
> in shining brightness and the place of truth. . . ."

A piece of paper, loosened among the leaves,
fluttered, yellow and brittle, the ink upon it
faded and brown. He took it up as gently
as though it were a butterfly. He knew
the holograph. It was Miranda Vail's:

"On the softest of turf, in this deep windless hollow
Where the barberry bushes are shining and bright,

Is the lost lifted up that my life seemed to follow,
In a new white flower that has bloomed overnight.

"Oh a new flower strange to this isle and enchanted,
Such as never on Kittiwake blossomed before —
By the lone seabird's rock, all my heart ever wanted,
Now at last, in my ageing, has come to my door."

He stared upon the lines, and as he stared,
urgency in the room was imminent
surpassing any he had felt before.
Rising, he said, "Are you determined on it ?
But why ?" and spoke to air. He took the book
and pamphlet reverently, and crossed the room,
and knelt before the fireplace, and laid them
on the made fire that he had never used.
Now the dark room was chill, not only with
the night, but with his loss and his dismay.
Who were the gods, to ask him if he knew
if he did well or ill ? He only knew
that what impelled him to it was as real
as human presence. So he lit the kindling
and watched the little flames creep and take hold,
and fixed the fire-screen fast before the fire,
and stood, head bowed, one arm along the mantel
in the dark room whose only light was this
where the blaze threaded blackened twisted leaves;
and knew the faith that he intended keeping
forever with the dead.
                              Then slowly, slowly
it seemed that heaviness was lifting, lifting,
and that great gentleness was golden round him,

and that a light was in the darkness, growing,
growing — that he was free, at last — and she
at last was free, who was Miranda Vail.

Note: Occasionally certain actual human lives exert such a ten-
sion upon the mind that the creative imagination is led to rearrange
characters and events, and to alter fact and circumstance for the
purposes of fiction. I have drawn here upon certain material in an
actual life, the atmosphere, a number of details, but only with the
most profound respect for the prototype of Miranda, and, indeed,
for a dead American scholar and student of Browning whose rôle
and nature are quite changed by the exigencies of the poem.

W. R. B.

V

NORTH SHORE

BALLAD OF A SHIP

O there sailed a ship of old called the *Young Marjorie*,
Her rigging all of gold and her sails on the sea
As the gull's wing white and as the gull's wing free.

She sailed to Surinam and she sailed to Ta-hi-ti,
She rounded Cape Discovery and tied at Cocos quay,
For a gallant ship and gay was the *Young Marjorie*.

Then she listed in the doldrums and she saw a crimson moon,
And among the archipelago she ran on a typhoon
That beat the sea to batter with a mighty iron spoon,

That twirled the sea in funnels and that span it hard alee
And whirled the tangled shipping to the dead Sargasso Sea
And left among the waterweed the *Young Marjorie*.

But the ship had such a soul as could calk her every seam,
The ship had such a spirit as needed none to bream,
The ship righted quickly, and sailed into the stream;

She sailed into the stream and she sailed into the sea —
And she wears a suit o' sail worthy better men nor me
And a figurehead that's magic on the *Young Marjorie*.

And in clouds above her fly all the birds that love the sea,
The petrel, gull, and tern, hawk and skua as they be,
The fulmar and the cormorant and plover of the sea —

In clouds of wings above her where she shears the billow white
They shield her sails who love her, sun of day and moon of night.
They clamor of the reef ahead, and carol of the light.

For her royals and her skysails have heaven in their fee.
She is yare to the whirled wheel, and dexterous and free.
O a gallant ship o' God is the *Young Marjorie.*

She will lift a fair landfall as all good sailors know.
She will ride out the worst wind that ever came to blow.
She will make the happy harbor where the surf is like snow.

The surf is like snow there, and azure is the sea,
And latitude and longitude by heart are known to me,
And of all the ships in roadstead so comely and so free
The brightest and the best is the *Young Marjorie* !

GRANITE SONG

The gull skims low past the rushing breakers,
    Low, low as the heart in me.
The gull lifts high to the wide sea acres,
    High, high as my heart would be.
The gull wing veers down the windy skyway
    Far, far, O far away and free.
With the last long gleam of the sun for highway
    The gull is out to sea.

White in the brightness as new snow driven,
On the curve of the world where the whirlwinds rise;
Adrift in the lift of profound blue heaven,
Or pale in the gale flitting storm-green skies;
In our granite grief, in our pain and our wonder
Beneath you on the grim grey rock we stand,
While you fly the lightning pennon of the drum-roll thunder
    Out of God's own hand.

The gull wing droops to the pounding breakers
    Low, low as the heart in me.
It lifts to the silver of the wide sea acres
    High, high as my heart would be.
It slants down a flaw of the windy skyway
    Far, far, O far away and free.
In the last long gleam of the sun for highway
    It is gone from the sea.

A BALLAD OF GLOUCESTER

Around the wharves of Gloucester
　　　That still remember sail,
Where men have fished for every fish
　　　From the herring to the whale,
Braving the North Atlantic
　　　In the coldest months of all
With barques and sloops and schooners
　　　And dories setting trawl,

I heard a chantey lifted,
　　　I heard a ballad sung
Of the days before the power-craft
　　　When the dory-men were young,
Of the white shoals of Georges
　　　And the fish that there abound
Though the freezing wind be howling
　　　Round the good fishing-ground;

Of the moving hills of water,
　　　Their hiss and rush and roar —
Rail awash for Boston lightship,
　　　With the sea on her cabin floor,
With the watch clinging lashings
　　　And the fo'c's'le sloshing foam,
But the crew all braced and shouting,
　　　From Georges driving home;

Running out from Gloucester harbor,
　　　Frozen herring aboard,
Bound for the Banks with the wind Nor'west,
　　　And their trust in the Lord;

Brought to in thirty fathom,
      And the fishing-fleet in hail;
All hands to furl the canvas
      And bend the riding-sail;

And, when they'd berthed and clubbed her,
      Their lines they hauled for cod;
Fine days in February
      And the fishing sent from God,
Till the glass was noted falling
      With a light spit of snow,
And the skipper's voice was bawling
      As he clambered from below:

"Heave in strads — give her cable !
      Loose the foresail and reef !"
Then hot coffee from the kettle
      And a chaw of salt beef,
And they're oiled-up and waiting —
      For blow she will and can,
With the seas cresting round them
      To suit a Georgesman.

There's a craft rising nigh them,
      And away into the gloom,
With faint voices that cry them
      To the creaking of her boom;
And may God help every vessel
      Gone adrift through wind and sleet
Where high seas and darkness wrestle
      With the Gloucester fishing-fleet.

Then dim daylight comes faintly
      On the crests of the breaking seas,

While the snow flurries gently
  Though it brings them no ease;
But the morning advances
  And the glass begins to rise
And they count upon their chances
  And they clear their weary eyes.

Armored in ice all for'ard,
  And the ropes and windlass too,
They crack on sail for Gloucester,
  With the fish frozen through:
The boys that haul and trawl 'em
  Where winds and waters roar —
May Death never call 'em
  But bring them safe ashore !

For the halibut and haddock
  Where the buoys stretch the skates
And oars stick up from dories
  To signal to their mates —
Where the staunch ships are anchored
  Or the trawls set under sail —
Or the hand-lines hook the mackerel
  In rain and a rising gale —

In the heart of freezing winter
  On Grand Bank or Banquereau
When the toughest hulls would splinter
  At the grinding of the floe,
As they saw some great berg passing
  Like a high cathedral white
With sun dazzling on its massing
  Ere it merged into the night,

They have told of a music humming
    In the lull of the crashing gale
Where a mermaid's harp was thrumming —
    Yellow hair and mullet scale —
Or against the fog-mull blooming
    From the golden lantern light
How one's shadow hove dark and looming
    As they dressed the fish by night.

But the ships that made that story
    Are lost on a winter shore,
With the *Greenleaf* gone to glory;
    Mary Burnham no more;
Men overboard from the *Ocean Belle*
    Or from the *Queen of May*,
On the Banks or on Georges
    Or the passage from Fortune Bay.

Gone down and lost in dories
    Out visiting their trawls,
Schooners of many stories,
    In sudden seas and squalls;
Mary Carlisle and *Gwendolen*
    In the gale of '79;
All through the years the ships and men
    And the lights that ceased to shine.

Men of the Port of Gloucester
    That looked on home no more,
Lost in the mackerel fishing
    On the Nova Scotia shore
Or St. Lawrence or Menhaden
    Or Maine or Malpec bar —
The Western Light — and the *Sparkling Wave* —
    And the schooner *Morning Star* !

BALLAD OF CAPE ANN

Champlain he left St. Croix on a cruise.
Heave on the purse-line of the seine !
His barque was filled with bait and booze.
Ho for the fishing of Sieur de Champlain !

He cruised a coast of rocks and trees,
He saw three islands off the main.
He hailed canoes full of salvages:
"*Parlez vous ?*" said Sieur de Champlain.

"Ze Cap aux Isles I name zee quick !"
He cried as he steered 'twixt wave and sun;
And he drew a map with a charcoal stick —
And that was Motif Number One !

He thought to discover the China Sea,
He was outward bound for far Cathay,
But the landfall he lifted was Gloucester quay,
And Halibut Point, and Sandy Bay.

He dined ashore with a Saco chief,
He calked his shallop on good Cape Ann,
And his soldiers nearly came to grief
When they ran afoul of a Rockport man.

He said, "Zis *place* it ees vairy good !"
He said, "I baptize it Le Beau Port.
Zere is plenty of water and plenty of wood,
And *soirée dansante* by ze shore !"

Then he sailed away with a spanking breeze
    From the brook, the marsh, the beach and the pine,
The wigwams of the salvages,
    The granite rocks and the purpling vine;

He sailed away into sunset fame
    From the three Turks Heads that John Smith found;
And he gave to Quebec a noble name
    But he never returned to Gloucester ground.

But *le Sieur de Champlain* was a haunted man,
    For never in Canada, France, or Spain
Could he find the equal of old Cape Ann —
    Gather the gill-nets — haul on the seine !

GULLS

The fishing boats are beset by a snowing of gulls.
The breakwater stands aloof, and the gulls go by,
are white on the water or darker against the sky,
and settle around the grey blunt-ended hulls.

The boats mount each a dory, rose-colored or green;
step each a mast; but move with a motored beat.
This afternoon they are more than a fishing-fleet
to the mewling gulls, those scavengers snowy-clean

that poise on their granite pulpit or rock on the billow,
that gather in caucus, pompous and dignified —
and then, with the boats of the fishers, where is their pride ?
They flutter the water like feathers burst from a pillow.

Yet lone as the gull-wing dips, and lone as they fly,
foreseeing the waves of the air that can lift or bind,
brighteyed and graceful familiars of the wind
they bend the great bow of beauty, slanting by,

lift my heart high, sway my blood to the sea,
are shafts of light in the sun, close kin to the wave,
and through changing colors of evening quiet and grave
wild spirits crying and flying forever free.

THE GOLDEN DUSTMAN

Song for a Sea Baby: M. K. B.

Down along the shore
you can hear the sea
whispering for you,
whispering for me;
blink of gold, blink of green
where the lights the night edge,
and the rustle of the surf
as it lisps on the ledge.
There's a path on the sea coined of old.
And softly and silently, not to be told,
with stars that like diamonds sparkle in the black
of the big velvet sack
that he bears on his back,
to the singing to slumber of stars beyond number
down the moon-golden track
comes the dustman of gold.

They say it is dust
that he casts in your eyes.
I know it is stardust
that renders you wise.
When wind, roaming and moaning
round our house in the night
like a wanderer who prays
for the loan of a light,
turns to sea where the long swell is rolled,
on the reef where the foam of the comber is shoaled,
then with stars coruscating in the depth of his pack,
in the big velvet sack

that he bears on his back,
to the sighing to slumber of waves beyond number
down the long golden track
comes the dustman of gold.

So you dream of the halls
that are under the sea,
that are glittering for you,
that are glittering for me;
and the kind lighthouse lights
fade from sight, out of sound
of the sighing of the surf
that in silence is drowned
where the white halls of coral are cold,
where the gay fishes glow and the seahorse is foaled,
where he pours out the stars from his deep velvet sack
till they blaze mounded light
where the caverns are black,
and the twangling to slumber of harps beyond number
make a new golden track
for the dustman of gold.

TRAMMELED SWIMMER

Sleek from silk water the angled arm. The sun
Shook crinkling sequins. Slipping ripples burned.
With thew and heart and blood and thought as one
      His body turned.

He twisted on his back, and at the noon
Thrashed sunbrowned feet; then lay, and let the bound
Of blue absorb him, like the faint day-moon
      A perfect round.

Floating infinity, for now the blue
Was cloudless, he was lifted to a height
No rock, no shore, no sea-horizon knew.
      He lived in light.

A Knowing profound; from all life's friction free;
Higher than flier; aloft, alone, elate;
One with all infinite possibility;
      Disjoined from fate,

And reaching almost . . . seeming about to reach . . .
He twisted prone; arm flashed and body sped.
"What were you swimming?" his friend asked, at the beach.
      "The crawl," he said.

GLOUCESTER SCHOONER

We were bathing from the granite when we saw her out on the blue
In the heat haze of September, hung between sea and sky,
White as the burgomaster gull to the fulmar or the mew,
Her hull that seemed of vapor and her lily sails on high.

Of the first of such from Gloucester, 'twas the word, "See how she
  scoons !"
Cried Captain Andrew the builder, "Then a scooner let her be !"
Two hundred years ago that was ! Her jibs made demilunes.
Aft to her main-gaff topsail she queened it over the sea.

She hovered and hove a phantom, and glimmered into the gray
Like the ghost of all Man's dreaming ere the End of the World was
  found.
Hardly she seemed in motion, barely to gather way.
Where was her port or venture, bound for what trawling ground ?

Only it seemed great beauty, ancient before our time,
That man could wed to nature when his heart and hand were one,
Paused like an apparition, in peace beyond my rhyme,
And, white as pearl on the sealine, ethereally was gone.

JORMUNGAND

Song for Foul Weather

Nostril-smoking, around the root
Of the dim Celestial Tree
He coiled, till Odin seized the brute
And hurled him into the sea.
Now is he bound around the world
As Loki harries the land,
And dizzy stars from heaven are swirled
At the heave of Jormungand.

To Asgard, and far realms, the roots
Of Yggdrasil extend,
And four white harts feed on the shoots
Of one at the world's end,
For there the Norns with muttering spell
Asperge the leaves from blight,
Though wisdom lies in Mimir's well
At the other end of the night.

At Niflheim great serpents dwell
In the ocean dragon's dearth,
And swung in space 'twixt heaven and hell
Is Midgard, or our Earth.
There till the Twilight of the Gods
Used Jormungand to be,
Till Odin found his worlds at odds
And hurled him into the sea.

Then round all seas his tail he curled;
And tempest and tide prevail

On all the coasts of the quaking world
When that he bites his tail.
The hurricane assails the main,
The tall wave walks the strand;
And Thor and Odin slay and are slain
By the fury of Jormungand.

The giants dwell in Jotunheim
West at the world's far edge,
Each with a great beard white with rime,
Each with a thunder sledge.
Their blazing eyes revolve in light
And Aesir's end they know.
Their weird is with the gods to fight,
Nine Worlds to overthrow.

And thus each fiord with fog is palled,
Rán's net afar doth fall,
Now Harald Fairhair's every skald
Is mute in mirk mead-hall.
The dragon beaks of the long ships drain
Far-thundering brine and spume.
Many-benched rowers strain amain
In Olaf's galley of doom.

For Ocean-Lasher, the Midgard Worm
Through all his length hath striven;
Haki's blue land declares its term,
Smokes high and leaps at heaven;
And with splintering oarblades on the strand
And wind that howls you dumb,
Hark the revenge of Jormungand,
For Ragnarok is come !

THE MORNING SHORE

Though a high surf roared heavily all night,
the waves shout in the sunlight, frothing white,
gathering along the rocks and spuming high in fierce delight.

With the great rollers cresting and curving home,
leaf-green alight in the hollow under the foam,
from the main deep dark blue-green, following on they come.

Gulls hover and plane, their blanched breasts and their gray
wings coasting. The raggèd goldenrod is gay
on the granite. In the deep-gashed gully shake white manes and neigh

the steeds of the foam. The candid sky washed blue
an exultation of sunlight in a new
bold day, now the roaring summons of wind and rain is through.

For all night through, the might of the wind and rain
screamed and shook affright on panel and pane
as the great guns of the cold northeaster blasted the main.

But now, all's blinding blue or blinding white.
The dazzling light forgets the dense dark night.
White foam spumes high on the ledges, shouting unwearied delight.

LATE SUMMER

When the aster's smoke-blue
And the mountain-ash is gold,
Many old things seem new,
Many new things are old.
There's a frost with the dew
And the first hint of cold.

There's Cassandra the crow
In a coign of the bay;
And the sun appears to know
What the surf seems to say:
That the lovers too must go
With the high wings away.

Lift your face to the sun,
Gray your eyes out to sea.
Past and present as one
In this pause seem to be,
With the new-born, long-done,
And the bonds on the free.

So the grief laid on you
Like a legend seems told
Where the old faith is new
And all new pangs are old,
When the aster's smoke-blue
And the mountain-ash is gold.

EQUINOCTIAL

The sea, in this late sun,
Has a salty glaze.
The aspen's leaves are white.
The pine sways.
In Autumn we are come
On tranced days;

Though wild the wind blows
And the surf below
Charges the rocks and throws
Clouds of snow
And as veil across the view
Makes the spray blow.

A veil on the distant town
The spray blows.
Houses white and brown,
Roofs in rows,
Steeples seeking God
The town shows.

The ridged sea in this weather
Singing home
Bears many a whitecap feather
And crest of foam.
Red vine, gold plume, on the headland.
Fall color has come.

White and brown gulls go over
And slide the air.
In the night, pulse of the lover

Wakes aware.
In the night one hears the surf
Growl in its lair.

One hears the surf say hush
Till dim of dawn.
Ever the rhythmic rush
And wave withdrawn.
Mortal metronome
I marvel on.

Life — death — life,
Death — life — death,
Obstinate strife
Of our defeated breath. . . .
Oh let the wild wind blow
That summoneth !

Blow, as to Paul, from Crete
Sailing on,
The prisoner of Rome's
Centurion,
Arose that mighty wind
Euroclydon,

Within whose roar and shriek
Through shroud and stay
He heard the angel speak
Before day —
Shipwrecked at last but not
Cast away.

Then I should know, should know
The bourne for those

Tossed high to light, who go
While their valor shows ! . . .
By the cliff, like an arm upflung,
The high spray blows.

VI

SPEAK WHAT YOU THINK TODAY

BRIGAND OF ELEUSIS

Swift came young Theseus on the mountain way,
climbing and striding, for the strength of youth
was in him, and the flush of victory.
His heart beat high and hard, as when he coursed
in hero company the tusked wild boar
that ravaged Calydon. His sandals took
the trail leaping and light. A boulder cast
a shadow across the road, whose other rim
dropped downward through the sky. With leopard stride
he rounded it. Then stopped. And stood like stone.

Here the road widened; and a structure loomed
of curious sort, a thing of iron frame,
windlass and thongs. It bulked beside the way,
yet hardly held his eye, for there behind it
one, even his experience of giants
found him unready for, was leaning backwards,
arms folded; and above his massive height
a face, like wrinkled granite of the place,
appeared in verity to attempt a smile
almost grotesque. From this disfigurement
a voice came, unctuous as oil, a voice
resonant on the rocks, yet suave and smooth.
"Ah, traveller," it said, "Ah, long-awaited,
welcome indeed !" But Theseus stood, and lightly
poised on his spread and firmly-planted feet
with thumbs in belt, and thought him of his sword.

"Aye, welcome !" cried the voice. "All are most welcome
who fare my road."

Theseus his voice discovered
to find it dry and thin, and hear it say,
"I am for Athens."

"Assuredly !" the other
rejoiced. "But break your journey here with me."

"No, you mistake," said Theseus, and his words
rang louder now around that coign of cliff,
"I may not linger. I am on a journey
the fates control."

"What talk is this of fates,"
rolled the gelatinous compelling voice,
"Fates ? Furies ? Phantoms ! Abysmal superstition !
Here I alone direct Man's destiny;
single ambition I halt, but serve the many.
I am the Equalizer. Do you see
this most precise machine ? It is a bed —
but not a bed of roses for vague dreamers,
nor yet a bed of down to rest the feeble,
and elsewhere you may seek the bed of love.
This is a bed of iron, making men
resolute, ruthless. It has metes and bounds
to regulate them all. This bed's foundation
is what you seek."

Into the oily voice
a sterner note had crept.

Then Theseus gazed
upon the iron bed that like a rack
stood ponderous with many rusty stains
on its unmattressed length and down its straight
short iron uprights. He endured the eyes
of the giant. He said, "I see your strong machine
of torture."

"Torture !" bloomed the oily voice,

"Not in the least ! What talk is this of torture ?
Here is solution of all difference.
This is the Equalizer. Rest and peace
for disproportion. This makes all things just
and fair, within one frame of regulation.
Let me convert you to my way of thought.
There is no other way. All other ways
are but chimaeras of a phantom freedom.
But you are weary, in your vain attempt
to reach some apparition, some illusory
place you call Athens. What you need is rest !
Rest and euphoria and utopia
and all men equal . . . ."
                    Something in the voice
was deadly as an opiate. Theseus swayed
upon his feet — then suddenly dashed an arm
across his eyes, and drew and gripped his sword;
and if the enormous image of the giant
wavered before him as though seen under water
yet he cried "No !" And the air all at once
cleared. He saw plain. He drew a breath as deep
as though he had been running at high speed.

"So-o !" said the giant; his rich utterance
edged with a crisper sound. "My friend, I fear
you are recalcitrant. You hug your own
base individual self with sinful pride.
You will not lay yourself upon this bed
for the good of all !"
                    "How for the good of all ?"
said Theseus.
            "The adjustments can be made,"
said the good giant, "O so easily !
by which you will approximate the norm.

Those levers and these wheels, and — er — that knife.
Indeed that is the long and short of it.
This is the Equalizer."
                    "Equalized,"
said Theseus, "in your fashion, I can see
small good for all !"
                    "Contentious !" cried the giant,
no longer with the smile that so disfigured
his strong and obdurate face. "We have a method
of instruction and persuasion."
                              And his arms
unfolded, and his heavy hands hung down,
and his prodigious fingers flexed themselves
and curled into his palms. Forward he leaned
as boxers wield the cestus.
                         Theseus took
an agile step aside, and Theseus said,
"I know your town wherein the mysteries
and doctrines to the initiate are revealed.
From here it is not far. And whether Iacchos
or Orpheos rule your rites, the sanctuary
raised to our universal mother earth
is there. I know the seed of future life
sleeps in the growing grain; that all things end
but in rebirth; I know the human vision
exists in only flashes of the light
against great darkness; and I also know
this engine here is nothing that the gods
decreed from their acropolis on high.
If it be not the gods, it is not best
on one strait bed to maim the body of Man
or on one doctrine to distrain his mind
so that all impulse of the thing indwelling
in all, can leap no longer on the road

toward the great city of Man, where all, together,
men work their own salvation through the mass
and toward the general good. You levy toll
of the human spirit for a deadly end
that, to your thinking, justifies the means."

The giant took one step, and the earth quaked.
He bent and spread his arms. He said, "Young man
You are a fool, a fool bemused by phantoms.
I am reality. I deal with facts.
I have no truck with mysteries. I know
the worthlessness of mysteries. I stand
here in my power, all men to equalize.
Weakling, do not dispute me !"
                                    Theseus said,
"No. You are unreality. You are
merely Man's dream of power. Man's dream of power
takes many forms."
                        The crouched colossus said,
with terrifying softness, "You are wrong.
I am what is to come. I am Mankind's
persistent destiny."
                        A paroxysm
twisted his features. He snarled, "I am the myth
that rules the multitude; the strength of greed,
the huge industrial will and enterprise
that maims all individual effort, making
the people mere automata, and wrenching
the work-slave to its measure. I exalt
power without obligation to the people
save by lip-service. I am the golden giant
you grapple in the dark. And, as I change
like Proteus, I am all of Man's beliefs
frozen to formalism, inquisition

of every heretic, being the rack
of all religions; and, out of noble dreams
of Man foiling his tyrants, I become
the father of coercion, the overhearer
behind all doors, the informer, the enslaver,
to one régime inseparably bound;
the sovranty of those who move protected
incessantly by weapons, whose word is death
since their reliance is not in faith but force;
the few that rule; the privilege that corrupts.
He who proscribes am I, and he who purges,
he who persuades the recreant to unmanly
abasement in confession, and loud babble
impelled by fear. For I am Fear itself,
Fear and Suspicion, and Hate that thrives on both:
Fear of all venturing on the open road
where their inquiry may displace my dicta;
hate of all highways paying me no toll;
hate of mankind evading me; drillmaster
of human thought; director of each impulse;
supervisor, even, of every instinct . . . ."

The lips frothed, but the small green eyes perceived
that words had gone too far. Nevertheless
the frenzy was upon him. "Those," he said,
"those who persist in hindering the creation
of my far better future for Mankind
will force me to erase them from the earth,
acting without false pity."
                                    Screamed the voice,
"To the bare compound and iron prison camp,
to the desert, to the snows with all of those
who spurn my generosity — who spurn
my pattern for the race ! The knife, the noose

for all who will not suffer my direction!
Death to the one who raises up his voice
to ease the ferment in his heart and brain!
I am as old as Adam, and as time,
as all intolerance, bigotry, and terror,
as folklore, law, and logic!"
                              Theseus said,
"Your words are whirled like leaves that feel the wind,
or as the incoherent voice at Delphi.
But I am he who moved the rock at Troezen,
I have my sandals, and I have this sword.
It slew the brigand who bent pine trees down
as I a twig, and bound a man between them,
and let them spring apart. Sciron, besides,
it slew, impersonator of a saviour
bespeaking victims with such honey mouth
that they believed a giant was a god
and when they hunkered down to bathe his feet
he spurned them from the cliff. This is the road
I take to Athens, to undergo my labours
as Heracles did his. I shall adventure
a labyrinth, and find a clue; reject
the hand that saved me; work much good and ill;
have Heracles for friend; and I shall lie
at last at Scyros. Meanwhile, I stand here
and you stand in my road. Out of my path!"

The giant laughed. The giant flexed his arms.

Then like a dragon rearing reared the sword,
flashed back in blaze, and quicker than the light
swept in an arc of shimmer; and it struck
and split the hulking monster's head, and clove
his body, breast and chine. The turbid gore

flooded the hero's arms. And from the rocks
all round, there suddenly arose a sound,
a gobbling chattering, an inhuman tumult
most horrible to hear, from all the maimed,
the broken in body and distrained in mind
that still survived the universal cure
Procrustes had prescribed. It was not laughter
and yet like laughter; and it was not hate
and yet like bile of hate. It buffeted
the blood-smeared rocks; the invective cacchination
was bruited from this hiding-hold and that
whence queer things peered. But westward in a sky
that had been purple storm, a slanting shaft
of sunlight wrought a haze upon the plain
below the mountain road.

                  Then Theseus leapt
across the giant's body, mired in blood,
and ran with his red sword, and put behind him
those cliffs of scorn, and turned beyond a boulder
athwart the path, and saw a mountain stream
cascading from the rocks above the road,
and stood and bathed beneath its glittering arc
clean of all soil; and, thrusting back his head,
gulped of its crystal torrent; and resheathed
his swordblade wiped upon the roadside moss;
then paused, descrying far upon the plain
tinted like amethyst in the quivering air
his destiny, glinting from wall and well,
temple and tower of Athens, near the sea.

THE CITADEL

What of Man's immaterial citadel
Less than the Word of God ? Who knew it well ?

Plato his Socrates;
The strolling talkers in the cool leaf-shade
Near the Lyceum, where the Stagirite
Who had taught Macedon, inquiry made
Through the organon into realms of light,
Into the perishing or the perduring;
And then, no less, that soul as Magnus known,
Albertus of Cologne,
Who taught the Angelic Doctor; yes, and one
Renegade Dominican with thought maturing
Whom the fanatic Act of Faith
Of the Holy Inquisition robed in flame
And stopped of breath,
Who was by Sidney loved, whose death was turned
Into truth's martyrdom, wherein there burned
The greatest truth he could proclaim:
Unity found in all the universe;
Immanens causa; a living mind to scan
The thinking monad, Man;
But since the monkish pedants were disavowed,
Miracles scoffed at, and most mysteries —
To secure a greater mystery than these,
And the soul immortal in the life to come —
Him they struck dumb. . . .
Copernicus confuting Ptolemy,
Not yet held worse
(By the same torturers) than troublesome,
Leaving his legacy

To Tycho, Kepler, to the moon-endowed
Pisan, wrought Galileo rack and prison,
Though from that soul's integrity arisen
"Eppur si muove !" cried. And, as he died,
On Christmas Day of that same ancient year
Light glowed in a small village in Lincolnshire
With Newton's birth,
Still the great man of science of our earth.

Thus did the citadel,
Whatever forces would torture and enchain,
Renew its faithful to strengthen and maintain
Truth in despite of hell.

Recall the other minds
That in their several kinds
Fought the same darkness backward, age by age,
In their indomitable pilgrimage;
Geometric Hobbes, bending so close to scan
Nature and Man
As to miss Heaven, but write *Leviathan;*
Verulam, father of much modern thought,
Conceiving science as a pyramid
Even as his predecessor did,
Rapt Roger Bacon, suffering prison and pain
for his burning-glass of mind
Lighting an old dark century; Descartes
Expounding science as a tree;
Locke for his part,
Advancing the understanding; holding well,
Even in the household of Achitophel,
The real though immaterial citadel.

The intricacy, the order, and the wonder
Of nature; the exploration of our thought

Wherein our cherished illusions come to naught;
Man's fate, ere his own impulse blast asunder
His world; control of the inordinate act
By reason; and ever — the fact, the fact, the fact !

Like cloud on a night sky
Great other names go by:
Proudhon, the cooper's son;
Quesnay, physician to the Pompadour;
The physiocrat Turgot;
Ricardo and Rousseau,
Swift and Defoe,
Glittering Voltaire, the analyst in Hume;
Franklin who seized the lightning from the gloom;
Kant, lost in space and time,
Impelling Hegel's climb
Out of duality into unity;
Dark Schopenhauer;
The Nietzschean lust for power;
All endless grapple with reality.
Godwin, and Shelley, and, as our age draws near,
Paine, the great pamphleteer,
Fourier, Henry George,
Marx — like a fiery forge
Shaking a continent, the image-breaker —
Darwin, who wrought
A deeper revolution in man's thought;
Bergson, new image-maker;
Calm consciousness of Freud
No flames destroyed;
Einstein of the vast theories that awe
And the all-inclusive law;
And others more —
Those other thousands, the ants with their ant-grains

And passion for research that shook their blood,
With only a few ever to understand;
The special seekers enduring through strange pains
To garner one small fact misunderstood,
Misread, and add it to a vast mound of sand
(Or seeming thus, until it shift to shape
A peak of knowledge no reasoning can escape.)

Accumulation where genius climbed and stood,
As when the young wife, pale and poor,
But intrepid the unapparent to explore —
As Marie Curie in uranium rays
Searching miraculous substance through a haze
Of surmise, at last cast wide a thunderous door
Into God's lightning-litten secret room
Where the least atom salvation holds — or doom.
Two physicists on a long eight-year road
Laboring in love together, till at last
The magical particle from pitchblende glowed.
That hour the die was cast.
Radium. Years passed. The atom in blinding light
Hurled utter annihilation from the height.

Atom of Man's salvation or Man's hell.
All of existence in the citadel.
Who hold that immaterial citadel ?

Philosopher, man of science, man of thought
Not to be sold or bought,
Though through the ages threatened and forewarned
And tortured and decried . . .
Unbribed and unsuborned
They labored till they died,
Each for his span
As light's frontiersman on heights still dark to Man.

No fetter and no fire
Availed to quench their infinite desire;
No tyranny, no death,
Inquiry ending only with our breath.

Now all is strange;
The range
Of life about us, minatory, immense,
Bludgeons the sense . . .
Yet hour by hour
Among the apparatus or strange machines,
Or high in the observatory tower;
By lamplight on the books, or on the screens;
By test-tube and through spark,
Current and wavelength, and all channeled power,
Enduring courage goes forth upon the dark.

GENTILITY

Dear delicate lady vaporous in your tea,
suave host with brandy and with bibelot,
calling a union-leader's name Legree,
shrugging of servants, "Really ! Well, you *know* — !"
remitting Negroes to the Old Plantation,
finding the Semite unfit to be your neighbor,
abhorring governmental regulation
since all industrial ills are caused by Labor;
fantastically there have come to me
old days in France when princes of the blood
"established practices of cruelty,"
their fine hauteur so little understood
that, if I told, eyes, lips what Oes would form !
Some feudal lord, returning from the chase,
commanded several serfs ripped up, to warm
his feet in their hot vitals. And a case
there was of hanging by heels before a fire
some wretched peasant to be relieved of pelf.
That was the old Burgundian desire,
the Orleanist's too — why not yourself ?
Ah, but you clamor and cry out on me !
You only wish the People in their Place.
How base my mind such parallel to see !
Civilization has advanced the Race.
Yet, by the portiere, while we sip our tea,
a quaint old horror really seems to loom.
Someone from a more outright century
grins like a wolf into the drawing-room.

MEN ON STRIKE

You say the President should not step in,
Sacrosanct Management not be touched at all. . . .
If they refuse to bargain, won't play ball,
And just sit tight because they're sure to win,
Because they have the money and the power
And to the labor argument present
Merely their boot-soles, reading, with evident
Obliviousness, the comics, hour by hour —

If they say merely, "This is what we'll pay.
If you don't like it, strike !" (that's what they say
In substance) you grow purple and deplore
Not *their* contumacy, but Labor's nerve.
"They got the bargaining that they deserve !"
But is that all Labor is fighting for ?

The real rock-bottom issue is as plain
As the plain people: a job at decent wage,
Without paternalism or patronage,
That meets the cost of living and can sustain
A family's self-respect; a decent place
To hang your hat; have children; under God
Make yourself more than a robot or a clod;
Be a real member of the human race.

Is that so much to ask, when corporations
Bulge with their profits and their bonds and stocks ?
What is it in the human mind that mocks
Fair play, till foul disaster shakes the nations ?
What is it that will not reason, will not plan,
Will not respect the dignity of Man ?

It costs so much to live; it costs so much
To raise a family. Above your head
Still hangs the old disabling human dread
Of age and illness. Others keep their clutch
On the employed because the unemployed,
Many and needy, persist on every hand.
Supply thus bountifully meets Demand —
The perfect balance that must not be destroyed !

Cheap labor and big profits, that's prosperity !
Let the rest perish or rot! Have no dubiety,
That's the old jungle law of our society —
Substantially, an eternal verity !
No ceiling on our prices, or the enjoyment
Of what we make — ignore all unemployment.

Sometimes, America, you seem to me
Typified by the gambler and the sport
of the Mississippi steamboat, with a quart
In his hip-pocket, and a fancy-free
Skin-'em-alive and wolfish gaiety —
The poker-player of that famed resort,
The old Last Chance saloon, still glad to thwart
Any approach to rationality.

You live in legend, you rejoice in myth.
Our highly-colored chimeras, how we love them,
Though a world starve ! But can we rise above them
Even to recognize as kin and kith
The homeless veteran, the mere man who bids
For a decent job to keep his wife and kids ?

Or will our manufacturers remain
Forever in the sport and gambler class

Trusting to luck on what they may amass,
Reeling like drunkards in a golden rain,
Repulsing, with cries of agonizing pain,
Demands from workers whom the system pinches —
System? What system? Do we grow by inches
Through endless years dwarf stature to attain?

Pontifically our journals of "good will"
Anoint and crown free private enterprise
And *laissez faire*. Has God in Heaven not eyes
To oversee and save his children still
No matter what they do, how deaf and dumb
They choose to be, till Atom's kingdom come!

Drone on, drone on, great editorial We!
Shout, huge advertisements, in all the papers!
Make monkeys of the strikers cutting capers.
They love to strike, enjoy to disagree!
They'd seize the plants, and don't know ABC
About the business. Of course they're always wrong!
They'd better get back and stay where they belong.
Say, isn't this the Country of the Free?

The Country of the Free! I saw the sun
Light endless fields of grain. I saw the bread
Of life destroyed while millions went unfed,
Unhoused, ill-clothed. I saw injustice done
Negro and Jew; heard apes in Congress rant
Age-old pernicious blather and stale cant.

The Country of the Free! Yes, a great land.
Thank God that I have known it East to West
And North to South, and still I love it best
Of all the various world the seas command.

I have known Americans of finest grain,
Honest and fearless, humorous and keen.
Beauty beyond all purchase I have seen
In the human spirit's eminent domain.

And shoulder to shoulder now I know they stand:
Our valiant dead and all our valiant living
To vivify with giving and forgiving
This Country of the Free, the impartial land
That it might be; with heart and mind and nerve
Its many-in-one to strengthen and preserve.

I will not see it a pen for bleating sheep
Watched by sly wolves; or, in the new dark ages,
Industrial feudal lords dispensing wages
Each from his fief and his baronial keep,
While small stockholders pull their caps and scrape
Their little crumbs of dividends together,
And are told they are the Owners, and wonder whether
They are caught in some strange nightmare past escape.

I will not think enormous trusts — and what
A word is Trust ! — can rack this land asunder
To disunited states, and harrow under
Plain human rights, all benefits forgot
Of human toil, of the great heart and hand
That bound the continent they call Their Land.

Land of huge fortunes and stupendous luck,
Landgraves, manorial lords, the privateers
(A golden sound in Israel Thorndike's ears !),
Railroads and banks and trusts that ran amuck,
Seizure of public earth, monopoly,
Titanic names like Vanderbilt and Gould,

Astor and Morgan, and other great, who ruled
For many a year the Country of the Free —

With all your passion for the picturesque,
With all your freedom for the Ragged Dicks
To climb, by industry or politics,
To wealth or fame, the picture grows grotesque
Now, in this age, when, whatsoe'er the weather,
We must fairly live together or die together.

Labor is a new giant ? Yes, it's true.
And, "What did you expect ?" seems a fair question;
And even if it gives you indigestion,
Are giants in this land so strange to you ?
"Captains of Industry" made quite a few;
The Oil King and the Banker and the Scot.
Giants must Have; The Others must Have Not.
How feels the foot inside the other shoe ?

Well, Gamblers, will you gamble ? Will you say,
"Let's really get together; join our strength;
Not waste in civil war ! The world at length
Is due for a big new housecleaning day.
For human rights — come on — let's stake our pride !
World, we are moving — all tin-horns stand aside !"

DEEP RHYTHM

To the American Negro

In spite of hate and fear and the scrawny hand
    of the ruffian on our land,
In what other land, to protest or to rejoice,
    have you so lifted voice
As here ? Distinct the utterance, clear and strong
    sounded in various song
From a great rhythmic race — as we have known
    the rich, the glorious tone
Rise and exult in velvet-throated chorus
Bringing your crucified palpably before us.

The dark musician of England, and in France
    the king of prose romance,
Russia's great fantasist, are noble fames
All yours, but here abide the thronging names
Of freedom's own; here oracles of fire,
    the clarion, and the choir,
Cleave like Ithuriel's spear the guilty night
    of men called white. . . .
Pride of our country, that freely, wing to wing,
With her white poets her dark poets sing !

THE IMAGES

No one spoke out. I looked upon their faces,
Their eyes withheld from nothing that they named,
The stiff thin mouth, lip curled against the graces,
The gaze remote, even from manhood shamed
And evil jubilant. In analytic
Distaste for the tormented and the weak,
They were absolved, the esthete and the critic.
They were superior. They did not speak.

The foolish died, the fond, the men of passion,
The ignorant, the befooled, the sorry press —
And burst the prisons of captives in that fashion;
And were tortured; and were mangled; more or less.
But here — here no one spoke. Not one warm word.
Not one warm human gesture. No one stirred.

There were those increased in goods and bland of feature
That having need of nothing yet were blind,
Wretched and naked, the tyro with the teacher
Of what it is that Man goes forth to find.
Gold they possessed, that never in any fire
Had yet been tried; raiment not far to seek
That yet was none; descended son from sire.
They were withdrawn, remote. They did not speak.

Wage earners died, the laborer, the hewer
Of wood, the drawer of water, serf of wage,
Factory drudge, mechanic, mighty doer
At forge, in mine; the clerkly, sad and sage.
These seated ones, from aught that had occurred
Looked up, looked down, looked outward. No one stirred.

There were those legislators grave and prayerful
(Earnest to prove the dead had badly planned),
Those of one lucky vote whereby their careful
Concern for us had not disarmed our land;
Now holier far than they who met the danger
With long foreseeing and vigilance of thought,
To his own past each shrugged himself a stranger,
Pursuing advantage still, by nothing taught.

These folded hands on amplitude of being
And took unto themselves a ripe increase,
Shredding all plans proposed, with sage foreseeing
That public hardship held the spoils of Peace:
God bless our Home, wheezed on the old harmonium.
(Please do not mention uranium or plutonium !)

Somewhere black bread and gruel were hard to come by.
Somewhere in rubble the rooftree of a home
Thrust like a gesture we recognize the dumb by. . . .
Somewhere a wooden ploughshare turned thin loam
And wet green paddies steamed, and skins were tawny,
And beggars swarmed in rags and picked their lice,
And wither-breasted mothers and their scrawny
And wailing infants chewed a little rice.

Expedient and predestinate aphasia !
Here was the feast, here each a Barmecide.
And what was Europe, what the East and Asia,
Or what, indeed, the rising bitter tide
Far nearer home. Demanding due respect
Sat ownership, anointed and elect.

Yet would an eye slide sidewise at another,
Betwixt thin lips the tip go of the tongue

Uneasily. "What are you thinking, brother ?"
Ran rat-like round the mind. These never young
Had never felt their blood in sudden riot,
Nor shared in Man's outrageousness or shame.
O that was certain ! They were too cool, too quiet,
Such dereliction never theirs to name.

And who were these, and what had done, deserving
This hell marmoreal, Hell could not break ?
Had they held course deliberate and unswerving ?
Had they turned anchorite for virtue's sake ?
One thing they seemed, in the cold mist confined:
Alien to flesh and blood and kin and kind.

When the Devil throve, their courteous voices never
Lifted above some decorous derogation;
Or else they ranted that evil triumphed ever;
But few could have surmised they had a nation.
Mankind they claimed; but when Mankind was stricken
Even to the soul, they looked fatigued and proud,
Fearing profoundly to feel their pulses quicken.
Their spirits wore an antiseptic shroud.

I know there is a horror worse than dreaming
In these emasculate women, clay-cold men.
In that I stood among them even in seeming
My human guilt was well rewarded then.
There, in my dream, they sat, each soul alone.
And no one spoke. And time dripped on the stone.

TRESCA

Who killed Tresca ?
Will we ever know ?
A free man, he used to go
throughout this land,
to learn and grow.

The workers knew
where his gage was thrown.
He laughed in Atlanta
at walls of stone.

He blazed with ire,
He loved to joke;
his long desire
was to free the folk.
He wrote and spoke
with force and fire.

I know the child
in the Christmas days
that the good giant
bent down to praise.
The blonde child bowed,
smiled and took
the great big hand.
Gravely, they shook.

"He makes bright Christmas !"
Tresca said,
who days later
in the street lay dead.

This has not changed
since life began.
The dark and deranged
kill the brave glad man.

Tresca loved food,
friends, women and wine;
the cruel he hated,
the cold hard swine.
I never met him
when his days were wild,
But I will remember
how he praised a child.

". . . So Mankind, confronted with the need for enormous imagina
    nation
Could not cope with the situation, and found nothing to do bu
    fight. . . .
Cold ? Well, all caves are dark and cold. . . . So . . . that . . . wa
    civilization. . . .
                Now do try to sleep tonight !"

VITAL STATISTICS

The statesmen bicker about the non-essential,
Press for advantage, pick the bones of the dove.
But though atoms of cataclysm are evidential,
In Trieste a boy and a girl are making love.

Legislators indulge in national rabies.
They ponder boundaries and bombs and guns;
But the Polish-Jewish mothers think their babies
As valid as the Bessarabian ones.

Mere men, we call the nations, are growling and warning,
Considering all they can get, not what they can give;
But in Oslo a workman looks up in the early morning
And thanks his God because his wife will live.

THE STRICKEN AVERAGE

Little of brilliance did they write or say.
They bore the battle of living, and were gay.
Little of wealth or fame they left behind.
They were merely honorable, brave, and kind.

THE OLD REVOLUTIONISTS

The Old Revolutionists plotted and fought and bled.
The New State came, and decreed that they must not riot.
Some, being rebellious, rebelled. . . . They are very dead.
        It is very quiet.

The Old Revolutionists dreamed of Freedom, they said.
The New State came, and planned according to plan.
On iron rules they laid a Procrustes bed
        For the spirit of Man.

The Old Revolutionists were an insurgent lot.
The New State came, and dispensed with toleration.
"Tolerate opposition ? Certainly not !
        We are building a nation."

The Old Revolutionists felt they were on the spot.
They had hated the prison and exile that they knew.
It was hard for them to conform. Then some were shot.
        Soon there were few.

Now there are none. But through the murk and the mists
A Workers' Millennium, surely to be achieved,
Shines bright as the one that the Old Revolutionists
        Saw, and believed.

SOUTHRON

I can go back to the room where the quiet voice is reading,
That body of steel and whipcord coiled in a leather chair;
And the gawky boy that listened, the half-grown boy, half-heeding;
     I can still go there.

Away from their black-belt venom, the hoarse degenerate hooting
Where they flog a "nigger" with wire, who would register his vote,
And befoul the halls of our Congress with slaver of lynch and shootir
     And the manners of the shoat.

For I heard the real South once, while the North was a noble saying
In that drawling voice remembered, that rang like a harp to truth.
Swine eyes and minds of murder, and the yellow dogs all baying,
     Were not of my youth.

Nor the balefire on Stone Mountain, nor nightshirt and mask th
    fired it;
Nor veterans lynched and blinded, and every murderer cleared;
The horrible farce of "justice," with fear and hate behind it;
     The thug approved and revered.

The latter-day pattern of yahoo my Southerner had regarded
As not clean enough for the kitchen, or where they scatter the corn.
That brilliant ironic eye, that fencing wrist that warded,
     Were otherwise born. . . .

For a moment forget the horrors, and hear the voice that is reading
With that little quiver of head because the phrasing is just.
Rank-breathing breeders of hate — that being their only breeding —
     Dwindle to dust.

reat ghosts of Lincoln and Lee moved through that room for an hour.
Mirth stood with honor and mercy, with virtue clean and fine.
have known a mind of the kingdom . . . of the glory . . . of the
power.

That much is mine.

SUBVERSIVE

Jesus Christ, who brought good news,
Talked in the Temple with fellow Jews.

The chief priests' question he struck dumb:
"By what authority art thou come?"

He spoke of the heir of the vineyard known;
The builders rejecting the cornerstone.

The rulers murmured, "He stirs the tribes!"
He was feared by the chief priests and the scribes.

Yet spy how they would, wherever he spoke,
They could not bind his words to the folk.

"For mine is not a God of the dead,
But of the living," Jesus said.

"Beware the long-robed scribes men greet,
Beware the synagogue's highest seat,

" 'Ware those who make long prayers for their ease!
The widow's house is devoured by these."

He said, "Great earthquakes yet shall be,
Famine and pestilence fearfully,

Portents from heaven, tyrants risen,
My chosen people cast in prison.

There shall be signs in the sun and moon;
Distress of nations falling soon;

The world in terrible danger taken,
The powers of heaven sorely shaken;

But though earth and heaven shall pass away,"
Simply He said, "my word shall stay."

Yet ever the chief priests and the scribes
Sought to kill him who stirred the tribes.

He said, "I drink no fruit of the vine
Till the kingdom of God be thine and thine."

He taught in the Temple, but took the road,
For the free wide air was his abode.

No edifice could hold in fee
The free man out of Galilee.

Sometimes I wonder, "Where is He ?"

Reading his word, the heart doth pine,
For along the page his footprints shine

Who walks in haste with a secret golden,
Speaking to us whose eyes are holden.

But when I hear, as their words defame him,
Furious formalists who claim him,

I think what He said at the dark ebb-tide,
"The Son of Man must be crucified."

Yet also he said, ere he hung on tree,
"I in them, and Thou in me !"

193

And so came to Gethsemane.

He prayed in the garden with anguished words.
The priests and captains took him with swords.

Those holding him, mocked with a loud oration.
They said, "This fellow perverteth the nation!"

The soldiers struck him and abused him.
The chief priests vehemently accused him.

He had drained the cup his Father poured.
He had said to Peter, "Put up thy sword."

.   .   .

What have we builded after this?
Edifice on edifice.

They may point upward to the sky,
But they do not always edify.

And now zealotic chiefs of men
Ruthlessly subdue again

Those who speak a word as free
As the stranger out of Galilee,

On whom they spy with steady hate,
Lest God be greater than the State.

Yet still, throughout the world, there stands
His house, that is not made with hands.

TO A DEAD MARINE

Your blood seeped through the black volcanic ash
on the pinpoint island where the dragon caves
crepitated and stunned with flash and crash,
      the whole beach ploughed for graves.

As the barrage roared over your platoon,
and mortar, machine-gun, rocket, and rifle-fire
made all your world like craters on the moon
      with fogging pyre on pyre,

you gripped the sand, and held, as you had held
in the Solomons, the Gilberts, the Ladrones,
till grim death towered over you, and felled.
      The island has your bones.

But when our flag from Suribachi's cone
spoke to the sky, its affirmation ran
for all mankind, not for one land alone,
      from Attu to Bataan,

and covering every ocean, east or west,
sunset or sunrise, yearned for, blurred by tears,
because your heart uplifted in your breast
      challenged the brazen years,

answered the lust for blood, contemptuous power
shaking the sword; fought, and returned again
to fight; and in one fiery earthquake hour
      proved men are more than men.

195

FAITH IN VICTORY

"Let us move forward with strong and active faith !"
The final words stand clear upon the page.
Having met all violence, survived all scathe,
Leveled the ramparts wherein the heathen rage,
Won from an enemy "whose destructions come
To a perpetual end," witness this Age
A new avowal from all Christendom
That on a mightier union we engage.

Words are but words — yet one word is a tower,
A rock, a fortress more than steel or stone
That the sorrows of death and hell shall not devour,
Though earth be heaved in graves and heavens lie prone,
Though His pavilion round Him be dark waters
(As we have known) and skies of furious light.
O sons of men, O Freedom's sons and daughters,
For no small thing you have triumphed in the fight!

Dead in your youth, you perished by the sword
While thunder shook the sky and tore the ground,
Yet wrought the will of one almighty word
Whereby the oppressor lies eclipsed and bound,
The world of Peace for every man and nation,
Not evil peace of tyrant and of slave
But a new ordinance for a world's salvation,
A covenant now to last beyond the grave.

Who can number the clouds in wisdom, or of heaven
Can stay the battles, or the unicorn
Bind to the furrow ? But to Man is given
Strength of the spirit no evil may suborn.

Say his Lord lives, that God-in-Man has spoken !
We stand above a dying Thing abhorred.
By our own hands the bow of steel was broken;
With hands that build, we shall break at last the sword !

WOUND IN SECRET

How are they divorced, cloven apart by war,
The heart and brain, that generous giant of flame
And that gray ingenious clerk in the pallid core
Of nerves and cells ! For nothing is the same
When will says kill, love stares in a black abysm,
And conscious cortex is set like a murder mine,
With duty damnation, and blood for the only chrism,
Till the spirit shrieks, like the mandrakes of Leah's line,
Torn from its rooted flesh. The soul is forced
By Amnon Death, till shuddering silence falls
And glare is ghastly on indrawing walls
Of the obsessive. O how are they divorced,
The heart and brain, till the inwardly bleeding and maimed
Grope toward love again, in a dark world crumbled and shamed !

THE SPECTRES

To the German People

Avidly would you seize
the hand of forgiving ?
What have you done to these
prisoners living ?

What are these kraals of dread
ghouls would disown ?
Great eyes of the living dead
turn you to stone,

stare, and burn to the bone;
nor can lip tell
what you whine to disown,
that is worse than hell

with a hand like iron to seize
on your croak for forgiving. . . .
What have you done to these,
the dead that are living ?

THE WAKEFUL NIGHT

What avail they, the vows you swear ?
        You have the same men:
the fearful in wrath, the opposer, oppressor, are there.
        They will oppose again.
    Will thy balk again in the hour of decision
    the people's voice and the people's vision?
Will they shrink the hope of the world to the ink of a scratching pen

What avail they, the battles you win,
        who are of the old mind ?
Morass of emotion you wander in,
        with all paths blind
    save — *O good, good, excellent past all measure !* —
    the path that leads to your greed and your treasure.
God, what came ye out for to see — what went ye forth to find?

What avail they, the plans you plan,
        who scheme the old scheme,
(nor ever for the good of Man)
        who dream the old dream
    of power and plunder, plunder and power,
    with your fear, and your wonder (in an idle hour)
at the arid desert the God-in-Man can make your kingdoms seem ?

The sacrifice in Bozrah — shall we see
        the same end ?
That the cormorant and owl and bittern be
        that last confusion's friend ?
That ye call on the noble of heart — and none agree —
but the satyr cry to his fellow by the felled tree,
and nettle and bramble clamber the ruined wall,

d the dragon pasture, the vulture settle on all,
here vainly we dreamed the tongue of the dumb might sing,
e wilderness silver with the waterspring,
d an highway be builded straight for blundering men
 fare on like fools redeemed, to fall not again,
d the sorrow and the sighing to flee away —
Hark to the clamor against the people's day
ing, how power fears for its overthrow !)
'hat of the vows you swear, the battles you win, the plans you essay,
the core of reason and truth, to shine like a lamp by the way, be the
   first to go ?

CHIEFTAIN

Now it is over. And since they desired
a world in ruins — behold, their ruin stands,
though the world's youth is fallen, and our sons
gave all to which their gallant souls aspired. . . .
Now we must build what is not built with hands
for a sick Earth whose naked hunger stuns. . . .

And in a garden by a deep slow river
all that was mortal of him who led us long
under the young green grass and April loam
is gathered to his country's heart forever.
From the large maples a rivulet of bird-song
makes twilight lyrical in the village home.

The whispering trees are dark by Haviland Pond.
Along the Old Creek road the shadows rise
till one by one the jewels of the night
in planetary mystery — beyond
our comprehension — cluster in the skies
whither late bugle echoes took their flight

after the hills had hearkened to the guns
in long salute . . . and on the White House lawn
far down the river and across the gloom
tall elms stand sentinel, the curtains drawn.
Nevermore may the pressure of his hand
touch the wheeled chair within the dark East Room.

We are challenged by his victory! He said,
"We must go on to conquer doubt and fear,
to end War's ignorant, barbarous scourge at last!"

"If we would build Tomorrow," the deathless dead
spoke, "in today's great planning persevere,
past party or faction, holding union fast. . . ."

The pen fell from the fingers, the tense breath
caught, the pain stunned — but the great mind and heart
to widening horizons high and clear
exalt our own — past the dark-ribboned wreath,
the flag-draped caisson, the fate that said depart.
In that white light we go forward without fear.

Though even now, with crawling plans and schemes,
desire for spoil, new mask and new disguise,
those work against us to weaken more and more
all we have fought for with our faith and dreams,
striving through boasted economic ties
to forge new weapons for some newer war.

O, armored then with more than arrogant might,
seeking the worldwide peace that he conceived,
even as we struck the manifest evil down,
to high responsibility of right
arise, great nation in whom his heart believed —
to the people's cause he cherished above renown !

AT WARM SPRINGS

In the room at Warm Springs,
In the house on the hill,
Something quietly sings
Lingering still:

Warm and loving thought
Of a brave heart,
That cannot be taught
By any art.

The cold and clever say
What was, or portends.
Their words will pass away.
Here were his friends.

Though by the blind reviled,
His hope for Man was one.
The crippled child
Smiled in the sun.

With valor his heart beat
Though War was a bloody cloud.
The tired man in the street
Looked up more proud.

Bold, many-sided mind,
Questing for all the door
From midnight blind
To day once more,

Here his heart is a shield,
The sunlight sings;
The crippled child is healed
At Warm Springs.

THE SONG OF TYRE

I the blind Phoenician sailor
   Saw great Tyre,
Watched the opal sea-mist veil her,
Sunset strike her towers to fire,
Heard her mariners' gusty singing —
Fleet feluccas race the night —
All that golden harbor ringing
   In the evening light.

Fashioned full of wealth and wonder
   Was that Tyre !
All her wharves were piled with plunder,
Gold and gear to a man's desire;
Babel of tongues and chaffer of trading
All along her clamorous quays;
Oar-banked galleys, lateens lading,
   Glamorous argosies !

Round her waterside carousing
   I praised Tyre,
Praised her dromonds' purple housing,
Swart Sidonians worth their hire,
Praised old Ptolemy's pharos glowing
When we lifted Egypt's land;
Praised great Solomon's temple, showing
   Jahveh's contraband.

With the wine in my eardrums ringing,
   "O great Tyre !"
Loud I hiccoughed through their singing —
Till like lightning flashed the dire

Bolt of premonition through me
(*Crackle of flames and rumble of wall!*)
And the certainty smote to me
      Of her thunderous fall.

On the hot breasts of my leman
      In dark Tyre,
I, the prophesying seaman,
Heard that Jew with God for sire,
Gaunt Ezekiel's voice declaring,
"Brimstone judgment, fire and flame
Fall on Tyre, whose deep-sea daring
      Only seals her shame!"

In the wine-shop by the water
Thus his cadenced accents came:

"I speak of Tyre the rock, Phoenician Tyre,
Tyre that is in Canaan, in Asher's land,
With Sidon to the north across Leontes, —
Tyre, her great king Hiram, sending David
Cedars, and cedar and fir from Lebanon
For Solomon's temple overlaid with gold,
Garnished with cherubims of olive wood
Within the oracle; and all the walls
Of the house round about with open flowers
And palm trees carved — Hiram who came from Tyre
To cast the pillars of brass and chapiters,
Covering the chapiters with pomegranates,
And stablishing the pillars of the porch
Lily adorned; who made a molten sea
Set with twelve oxen like a brimming cup,
Filled with two thousand baths; and brought to being
The House of God for Solomon the King —

206

Hiram of Tyre whose cloudlike navies sailed
Bringing to Solomon gold from out of Ophir,
Apes and red sandalwood and precious stones;
Tyre that was proud, the place of perfect beauty,
With all its shipboards fir trees from Senir,
Their masts great cedars, their oars of oaks of Bashan,
Their ivory benches of the Ashurites
And out of Chittim's isles; their broidered work
From Egypt on fine linen sails with blue;
Mariners from Sidon, ancients of Gebal,
Wise men her caulkers, ships of the Great Sea;
Persians her men of war, and men of Lud
Hanging the shield and helmet up to her;
Javan, Tubal and Meshech at her fairs
Trading the mould of Man; Togarmah trading
Horses and mules, and horns of ivory;
With Syria her merchant of fine linen
And broidered work, and emeralds, and purple,
Coral and agate, honey and oil and balm;
Iron and cassia and calamus from Dan;
And lambs and rams and goats from Kedar; spices
And precious stones from Ramah; and to her
The ships of Tarshish sang. She was replenished
Gloriously !
   But on her fell the Doom,
On her the irrecoverable fall;
God's wrath for her idolatry; His fire
For what her ancients wrought within the dark
Each in the chambers of his imagery.
So now her towers and her suburbs shake
And all her pilots cry out bitterly
Casting dust on them, girding them with sackcloth,
Saying, 'What city was like to Tyre — what city
So glorious, so fallen ?' All the Isles

Shout with astonishment, and all the merchants,
And all the Princes of the Sea come down
And lay aside their robes, and sit and grieve,
Taking up lamentation, saying to her,
'Oh how art thou destroyed who wast renowned
Of all seafaring men, a luminous city
Strong in the Sea ! Now shall the Isles tremble
In the day of thy fall; for thus saith the Lord God,
"I shall bring up the utter deep against thee.
The waters shall cover thee. For as wolves ravening
The evil Princes came, the sound was heard
Of their dominion; and the great King of Tyre
Cried 'I am God, I sit in the seat of God !
Behold I have great riches with my wisdom
And by my traffick have increased those riches
And am exalted !' " Therefore saith the Lord God
'Since thou hast set thine heart as the heart of God,
Behold therefore I bring the strangers on thee,
The terrible of the nations. They shall draw
Their swords against thy beauty, and shall dim
Thy brightness. Oh thou son of man, take up
This lamentation upon the King of Tyre:
"Thou hast been Eastward in Eden, in the Garden,
With every precious stone thy covering:
The sardius, topaz, diamond and beryl,
The onyx and the jasper and the sapphire,
The emerald, the carbuncle, and the gold,
The workmanship of tabrets and of pipes —
And thou hast walked upon God's holy mountain,
The holy mountain of the beauty of God,
And up and down in midst of the stones of fire —
Ere by the quantity of thy merchandise
Thine heart was filled with violence, and thy reason
Corrupted, and thy sanctuaries broken

By the multitude of thine iniquities.
Therefore I bring forth fire in the midst of thee
Fire from the air and ashes on the earth,
Blood in thy streets and weeping in the dust
And the sword judging upon every side,
That if men ask of Tyre that once great city,
One shall reply: 'With Egypt desolate,
With great Assyria fallen ! For her rowers
Brought her into deep waters, the east wind
Brake her asunder in the midst of the seas
That now she lies a bare and barren rock
Only the white wing-wafting seagulls seek
To perch on and defile, and mariners
Know only as a place for spreading nets
To dry in sunlight under a blind sky !'

Clattered the wine-cup from my grasping
   In dark Tyre;
Shuddered the harlot from my clasping;
Stared and glared mine eyes on fire
As I sprawled the table, muttering
"Fallen, fallen, in all her pride !"
While the wine-den's lanthorn guttering
Cast its gleams upon the tide. . . .

Later, through thronged noon I stumbled
   Streets of Tyre.
Suddenly my heart was humbled
And mine eyes were seared with fire . . .
While the prophesying shook me
Like a burning desert wind,
Vast enveloping darkness took me.
   I was blind.

Therefore I, the ancient sailor,
           Tell of Tyre !
Still I watch the sea-mist veil her,
Sunset strike her towers to fire,
Hear her mariners through my dreaming
Chanting 'mid her sails and spars —
Myriad lights at anchor gleaming
To Night's myriad stars !

VII

HIGH FANTASTICAL

IMBRIUM MARE

"A so-called sea in the northeast
quadrant of the moon"

Is there rain on Imbrium Mare ?
Is there light ? How late, how soon ?
Do the waves of Imbrium Mare
Trail the frozen beaches of the moon,
Those pale forlorn far reaches
Where the mind's rare creatures play
As the foam of Imbrium Mare
Floods caverns of a phasmal bay ?

In the dark I breathed *Imbrium Mare,*
And a light came through the gloom.
All the ghosts of Imbrium Mare
Were there in the moonlit room;
And the image of Imbrium Mare
Was a danger for my feet
Where it wavered like a veiling
On my eyes in the hot bright street.

Who lulls me from Imbrium Mare —
Ah, what phantom from what wave ?
Where in foam-fire Imbrium Mare
Lost dreams their garments lave.
O breathe not *Imbrium Mare*
Lest your heart know the truth too soon
Of unfading Imbrium Mare
In the far dark quadrant of the moon.

THE BESTIARY

Contemplate Pliny's Crocodile
that had foreknowledge of the Nile
its yearly rise, to hatch in peace
its eggs as large as eggs of geese
wherefrom no creature, land or sea,
"groweth to bigger quantitie."
Thus of the female, while the male,
tongueless, but arm'd with claw and scale,
his "never twinckling" eyes fixed grimly,
(though underwater "they see dimlie,")
upon the desert crept for slaughter
all day; all night, beneath the water.

View here what Poets seek in story:
Comparison and Allegory !

Dentes prominentes et ferratos
runs one of Aristotle's mottoes,
to say no living beast had both;
And yet so Crocodilus doth,
Pliny averreth, who tells what foison
of deadly office had its poison.
Aquatilis et fluviatilis —
Or air or water, brunt of battle is
the life-breath of the Serpent-bred,
though in the sun they lie like dead
and though Ile Tentyrus' small men
both rout and ride them now and then,
forcing a wedge betwixt their jaws
they may not reach with their short paws.

The Trochilus, a tiny bird,
did cleanse their jaws of meat and curd,
yet, by sharp thorns upon its head,
obstruct that Crocodile be fed
ingratefully upon its friend !
Natheless this bird its time would spend
in friendly office almost human
preventing entrance of Ichneumon
into vast Crocodile's great maw,
sun-drowsed as he deep breath would draw
in slumber. For this Pharaoh's Mouse
would then, like thief invading house,
steal down his throat and burst his heart
by preying on each vital part,
whereat the dragon, wallowing deep,
would with great mourning sigh and weep,
and roll and toss and throb beneath
those unpacificable teeth
that scored like doom and fire, I tell ye,
with fell Ichneumon in his belly !

Trochilus, to avert that savage
invasion and ferocious ravage,
would squawk at sluggish Crocodile
to wake and meet th' assault of guile.
"But whether this be true or no,"
Strabo they credit for saying so,
as other scholiasts kept in view
what things the Ethiop dragons do
in multitude their tails that knot
together, spreading round one spot
to trip, with ruth and kindness scant,
the heavy feet of Elephant
their mortal foe; and thus they told

of fabulous Cockatrice of old,
as Lemnius saith, and with what risk
he did affront the Basilisk;
or how the Rhoetians, or Boeotians
who caused such dolorous commotions
against the army of Lysander,
spake of the mottled Salamander:
as how a human, by it bit,
as many spots as are on it
would learnèd chirurgeons need;
or how the Unicorn is treed
on the palm-trunk, by horn stuck fast,
whereat the Lyon laugheth last !
Or Gorgon beast of Lybian sort
whose glare decrees, like trump, the mort,
surpassed in horror scarcely more
by lion-footed Manticore
with treble teeth, or, as may be,
Mere-man and Monsters of the Sea
as Burchualur's huge horned head
and Whales, with scales, like Iles of Dread. . . .

But O the astounding River Horse,
his tail entwinèd as a Boar's,
his hoof as cleft as that of Cow,
his Horse's neigh, and tusks that bow
all crooked down; his skin or hide
like targe that all Man's darts defied !
He squattered through the Nile in mail
to gnash on Crocodilus' tail
and froth the stream to bloodied yeast,
the while the bellowings of each beast
blew up such clouds of yellow sand,
in that incandent Eastern land

snaked through by emerald ancient Nile,
as now blot Pliny's Crocodile
and all its epoch from our sight,
leaving the Sphinx to orphic night.

WHITE MAGIC

Now if I
as I asked you, go
where there lie
leagues on leagues of snow
like a feathery garment fallen
or immounded rondures frozen
of the chosen flakes that faltering
frost the long
fence row,

I afoot
while I lurch
and lift
heavy boot
through the drift
on drift
feeling cold within my nostrils
sharp and stinging on my eyeballs,
wintriness like brandy burning
as the blowing
needles sift,

I alone
in this catafalque of white,
in my own
alabaster cave of night,
lacking you not understanding
how the need was for my going
and my knowing doomed aforetime
with the light
still light,

wish you all
of my circumstances known,
though I fall
failing on my search alone,
when the solitude demands you
and your eyes are wide and staring
and no hearth or home can hold you
and the buffeted
door has blown

wide to white
and a silence that will grow
with the night
that enlarges all below;
for your leaping heart will tell you
why it needed me to vanish
through the ghostliness
of nightfall
and the whispering
of the snow. . . .

SNAIL

Let the distempered rail,
The sour of tongue decry;
Observe the mantled snail
Devise a silver trail
To chide the sessile eye !

Mark how it casts about
For God or leaf of green,
Though anger score and rout,
Though guile whip in and out
To mar the garden scene.

Though gibe cry "Jay, jay, jay !",
Bright fruit be spoiled of flies,
See Snail through tedious day
Reluctant silver lay
To foil hate's golden eyes.

MELISTORTE

In that strange land hight Melistorte,
Like the gray rampart of a fort
Rose before my riding eyes,
As my courser took the rise,
Winding walls of goodly size.
With fields white-blossomed all about,
What was it that those walls shut out ?
Dust from my horse was still adrift
When I beheld blue mountains lift
Behind the walls. And then I heard
Clear chuckling lyrics of a bird
Rippling with tone like that which flows
From a gold harp's arpeggios
Venturing various essay —
Then full flood music — till the day
Dizzied while that music ran. . . .
Midway the walls a barbican,
Grim of towers, yawned its gate
Through which we seemed impelled by fate
Into a fresh pleasaunce of flowers
Breathing ease and languid hours
While, for its influence, the air
Of fragrance seemed the thurifer,
That flowed around and over me
Till I was drowning in a sea
Of perfume. Then my steed stopped dead,
Shuddered his length, reached down his head.
I saw them coming from their bowers.
Women they were, and yet like flowers,
That soon against my saddle pressed
Lovely face and buoyant breast,

Shoulder and arm of such contour
Consorts with sylphic paramour.
To their terrestrial paradise
They welcomed whom they would entice
Deeper into redolent groves,
Laughing, murmuring of their loves.
There from hidden conduits flowing
Wine was golden, wine was glowing.
One drew me down upon the sward
To deep delight. I could not ward
Away her swift and smooth embrace
Nor the wonder of her face,
But held her wildly . . . Deep on deep
I sank then to surpassing sleep.
. . . My limbs were lead, my soul was slain.
Everywhere an arctic plain
Salt and white and cold within
Seemed to the earth a shrivelled skin.
And over me, against green stars,
Two giant slaves or janizars
Made waking wince with sharp command.
Attending me on either hand,
We trod the mountain to a door,
Traversed a cold marble floor,
And entered a great room of state
Where that old Sire of Darkness sate
Who rules the realm of Melistorte.
Corrupt in age, he held his court
Creating murderers of those
Mad to retrieve the fervent throes
I first had known. And I remember
In that copper-glowing chamber
Those who stood along the wall
With dreadful eyes, nor spake at all;

Those who had slain for him, ere this;
Whose dry lips chewed the cannabis,
Drugged and doomed by their desire
For gardens now turned gaols of fire,
For bowers and bosoms of such ease
As Nessus wrought for Heracles,
The robe smeared with the centaur's gore
That clung, and stung whomever wore
Till madness blazed. At this assize
Murder smiled with guileful eyes
On me, yet spake with wistful air,
"Warrior, wouldst thou repair
To that elysium of delight,
To woman, nightingale, and night,
Verbena fragrance, attar of rose,
Where a moon all golden glows
On silver fountain's gauze of spray ?
One I would have thee put away,
Slaying for me mine enemy —
Wouldst thou destroy him, or be he ?"
That venerable infamy
Breathed with a velvet voice that stole
Like numbing venom to my soul. . . .
O then her breath seemed as my breath,
Her embrace the foil of death,
Her beauty bathed in heaven's light;
Torture by her, benedight;
Memory of her, palsied trance;
Her body and her countenance
Like long desired and dawning day.
"The weapon !" I heard someone say
Hoarsely, 'twixt a sob and groan. . . .
And knew the utterance for mine own.
Then, for its echo, a grating sound,

Like metal upon granite ground,
Those brazen walls I heard engirth
As the Assassins tried for mirth.
Was it that sound that woke in me
At last the deeper memory ?
Sudden it flared; and I could see
As through a tube, a round of light,
And a small picture clear and bright
Wherein wine cups tossed at feast
Of kings and princes of the East
While execration shook the skies
"Drink ! For now the foeman dies !"
The curled flesh of mine ear could hear
Trample of armies thudding near,
Whinnying of beasts, accoutrements
Clinking and jingling from the tents,
Loud shout of orders, taurian blare
From wound bronze horn, and wild fanfare.
And straightway I recalled, dismayed,
How one vedette by night had strayed
And lost his way, and come by day
Toward great inhuman walls of gray:
One outpost of the Horde, whose trust
Now in his mouth was ashen dust.
I thought, "But they should not be far
If this be in their path of war,
Nor for one hour these walls should stand !"
Then saw the weapon in my hand,
And, on each side, like iron bars,
The great arms of the janizars
That held me. High above me doomed
The Old Man of The Mountain loomed
Leaning forward in his seat,
Flame red robed from head to feet,

Wizened death-face bearded gray,
Snake eyes glazed, that candid day
Had not shone upon for years;
His thin-lipped smile was worse than fears
Or howling wrath or menace grim.
I stood, and shook, and stared at him.
When sudden on silence came a sound
Pattering and gasping. With one bound
A loinclothed figure leapt the room,
Fell prostrate at the throne of doom,
Then raised his head, and wailing cried,
"The Tartars !" — writhed, convulsed, and died,
Swallowing his tongue to fend worse death.
I heard a hoarse and shuddering breath
Come from the throne, then a great shout,
"To arms !" And I was wrenched about —
And loosed, by my stampeded guard.
In the high door, red-scimitared,
Backed by a muttering press of men
Who rent the tall gold curtains then,
Horn-helmed stood that gigantic man,
My father, captain to the Khan.

HERMETIC

He bowed there at his dim routine,
His cavern lit with green and crimson,
The wizard of a twilight scene,
The Trismegistus they make hymns on.
Apothecary-priest of pestle,
Within that mortar he could bray you
Peculiar herbs that from his vessel,
Slipped through your veins, might well repay you.
For he knew shrubs, and herbs, and roots;
With all exotic plants was handy;
Divined the use for Upas shoots
And Pernambuco jaborandi.
Far more than mere pale pharmacist,
Filled with the whole pharmacopoeia,
Worse ills he had upon his list
Than glands or Sydenham's chorea.
Behind that intervening pane,
Before the counter where he tarried,
His hands had but to stray again
From jar to jar, and balms were married,
And strange ingredients once wellknown
From peaks of Ala Dagh to Mayence
Entered at last into their own
Beyond the grasp of modern science.
Thus pentagrams upon the glass
Appeared, and signs of old magicians.
I saw the summoned spirits pass
To their hermetic fixed positions.
There Samael, Oriphiel,
And Raphael and all the others
Glittered and stood; and miracle

Made all the patients feel like brothers.
With sulphur, alum, scammony,
And other subtle perfumes wreathing,
Alien to any gammon, he
Wrought magic cures as quick as breathing.
For there he plucked a yellow vetch
To pound it up and add unto it
Flower of the stylewort. . . . Lo, some wretch
Was quite rejuvenated through it !
Why, paralytics found their legs;
In roaring health, the merely queasy
Went juggling casks and heavy kegs,
His potions made their strength so easy !
Yet poisons of insidious flame
He could have brewed; a fit conniption
Might have bestowed on one who came
With benefit of no prescription ! . . .
I jerked from dozing in the chair
(O Morpheus, how close thou huggest !)
I started up, too late aware
I'd had a cat-nap at the druggist.
Subdued, dissembling like a fox,
I paid him (though I spoke in whispers),
Then took my little cardboard box
To join the homebound world at vespers.

THE LITTLE CATS

Our mackerel cat
Has three kittens.
The girl one sat
With white mittens
Down in the hall.
The grandfather clock
Bonged. The kitten
Shied at the shock.

Pounce, bounce,
Come her two brothers.
There were once
Three others.
We don't surmise
Who their sire is.
Their round eyes
Are all iris.

They sleep in a ball.
They scuffle and scamper.
Once they lived all
By the clothes-hamper.
Of their mother they know
They can't boss her.
They sit in a row
For the milk saucer.

They think a brown marble
Is a mouse.
They hop up stairs
And lurk through the house.

Pretentious books
By many are written.
I prefer the looks
Of a high-tail kitten.

THE BIG FELLER

Judas ! He give sech a shout
he jounced Gawd's cheaters right off'n his nose 'at was peerin' da
    through the sky.
He tuk'n scaled off the roofs from th' houses all raound about
an' ruffled th' rumps of a hull passel uh angels featherin' by.

He whooshed her up mooin', an' tuk a big tug at the teats
of the caow thet jumped over the moon. By gravy, it war quite a cape
It blasted th' little critical fellers all aout uh ther schoolroom seats
an' hed 'em daown all over th' floor scrabblin' fer pencils an' paper.

An' he sez, with th' milk uh th' moon drippin' stringy-white on
    beard
an' his furrud ablaze like the sun, "Wa'al, up 'n N' Hamshur, th' say
thar's scholards thet calls fer World Guv'munt, seemin' afeared
of sumpin' 'll happen ef I sh'd git started t' go on my way —

"An' they better be skeered, an' go grab up ther goods an' ther treasu
fer sure as plutonium, sartin as kilowatt hell
ye caint keep me hid — an' ther ain't no counter measure !"
An' with thet, sir, he lets out a yell. . . .

It splintered the high white steeple uh th' high-toned 'Piscopal chur
an' it whisked the hoorhouse down in the holler right off'n its foun-
    tion,
an' all uh th' settin-purty people felt like they was left in th' lurch –
but th' poor bad people, they thought it was Day o' Salvation !

Then he stud with aams akimber, an' he squinted up t' th' sun,
an' he sez, "Hi, Paw !" An' he give his big red galluses quite a hitch.

230

An' he leans up agenst a mountain, picks his teeth with my old shot gun,
n' he sez — etcetera, endin' "Well I be a sunnavabitch !"

He hed one foot over behind Old Baldy, one down in our own South
    Forty,
n' hulkin' above the wood lot he war seventeen times ez high
z th' house, an' th' glarin' shuht he woah war suttinly suthin sporty;
n' he spit in th' eye uh th' sky.

An' he sez, "It's a laff ! Thar's the scientists tellin' 'em true,
n' th' guvmunts shakin' an' quakin' an' duckin' an' dodgin' fack,
vile right under ther eyes is th' ackshal end uh Creation come true
n' dumb human nater's big disappearin' ack.

Will they go fer One World, er a great big armyment race ?
Vatch now — watch big industry tryin' ter handcuff 'n hide me !
Vatch ther tiny picayune fellers scurry over th' body an' face
h Gulliver-Me — wide awake, with th' Secret uh Bein' inside me !"

Val, sir, I watched him from whar I was layin' roun' back uh th' baan,
n' he stooped like a total eclipse, an' he shuk suh I knewed he'd fahnd
    her
vhar she glittered dahn in th' dust. . . . Well, he snatched up thet
    Gabriel Haan,
n', like no one but he cud, he wahned her. . . .

An', lissen, they was people stunned by it a hunderd mile away.
They seen all the winders was starred an' bruk, an' thought Gawd was
    aht t' scat 'em;
n' he bellers — tuh nubuddy standin' rahn, "Ef ye didn' wan' Jedge-
    ment Day
vy in hell-an'-all didja git me outta th' Atom? "

An' then, I seed haow Gawd hed ben makin' th' heavens awful blac
But thet big feller grins like a rosy sunset; he winks like a star at me.
"Hang on ter yer good green airth !" he yells. "But watch out ! I'll
    comin' back !"
An' he vanishes, like a waterspout, aout t' sea.

BALLAD OF A BALLAD-SINGER

John Lomax searched for folk song
Under Southern boughs,
'Mong the pickers in the cotton fields
And the singers in the barrel house,
And road gangs heaving hammers high
To a work song with a golden cry.

Down in Louisiana
The convicts sing long.
Though prison walls are high and gray
Their halls are stored with song.
Such wealth John Lomax found at last
Where shackled Negroes shuffled past.

In a cell at Angola,
Marked by stripe and bar,
There sat the self-acknowledged king
Of the twelve-string guitar,
And he could sing as long as you please
To charm the birds right out of the trees.

He was big and he was black
And wondrous were his wrongs,
But he had a memory travelled back
Through at least five hundred songs.
When his fingers gave those strings a twang
Like a very god in heaven he sang.

He sat there in his stripèd suit,
He sang like Kingdom Come.
At the end of day, when his voice was mute,

John Lomax sat dumb,
Then wrung his hand without a word
For the marvellous ballads he had heard.

And Lead Belly said to Lomax,
"I have written a song
For a pardon from the Governor,
Since my sentence is long;
As I sang to Governor Neff of late
When he pardoned me from Texas State.

"An' if so be I might request —
Put that song on a roll,
An' let the Governor hear it
So he may save my soul !"
And they made a record of his petition
And pardoned him on that condition.

And Lead Belly came to Lomax
In the fall, as it befell,
When he was sitting in the lobby
Of a Texas hotel.
With knife, guitar, and sugar bag packed,
Lead Belly stood there, for a fact.

"Boss, I killed, without my fault,
For it was an attack.
They jumped me, and I tell you, Boss,
I had to fight back."
Said Lomax, "So ? Well, here you are,
And I need a driver for my car.

"But if some day on a lonely road
That knife of yours gets free — !"

"Oh, don' talk that way, Boss,
Don' talk that way to me !
If anyone tries to do you dirt,
I'll take the bullet before you's hurt !"

Lead Belly drives the Lomax car
And he is never tired;
He's a better man, John Lomax vows,
Than any he ever hired.
He sings at prisons to convict throngs
And helps John Lomax gather songs.

Just as folk strip Southern grapes,
Muscadines, scuppernongs —
So, from the heart of all the land
John Lomax gathered songs;
But in swampland Lead Belly he can scan
A whole book of ballads all in one man !

So here's to the man of folk-lore
And to Orpheus his peer,
With a voice that makes brown ladies swoon,
And a scar from ear to ear;
And, I hope for Lead Belly's sake, a charm
That will protect him from all harm !

Once in an age a minstrel
Like Lead Belly doth arise,
And then it's good to hear him singing
The stars right out of the skies
With his own "Bill Martin — long and slender —
Better known by bein' a bartender !"

BILLY BOWLEGS AND HIS MUSICAL WHALE

All the reaches of the beaches of the ocean in a gale
Roar the song of Billy Bowlegs and his Musical Whale

Every finback, or rorqual, or sulphur-bottom sail
To the tune of Billy Bowlegs and his sweet-spoutin' whale.

Every sailor on a whaler when they brailed the mainsail
Made the shanty Billy Bowlegs and that double-reeded whale.

Heavy laden with menhaden, all the coast fishers hail
That hoss-mackerel cowboy an' his tootin' sparm whale.

Fer he come from Wyomin' whar he rode on the trail
Callin' "Which way's the wagon ?", fer he longed fer wassail.

He was king o' bronc-busters an' he rode the rough string.
High-roller, gut-twister, say they didn't mean a thing.

Sulker, spinner, sunfisher, he forked many a killer;
An' he balled up in fallin' like a rele armadiller.

Every belly full of bedsprings that proud puncher sat
He'd yeow, "Pow-der River !" an' be fannin' on her fat.

But they say thar was a lady, O they say thar was a jane.
She come from Massachusetts on the Oveland train.

So that peeler was hog-tied before he began,
She had him choked speechless with a fast hooley-ann;

He left old Wyomin', an' he come to Cape Cod
Whar there's schooners an' mackerel and big fish, by God.

But he pined fer the grizzlies, an' the cavvy an' corral,
An' a bronc walkin'-beamin', an' a pirootin' pal;

So he pals with the fishermen that rocks on the wave,
An' he washes off the war paint, an' gits ready ter shave.

But out fishin' one evenin', with the waves gittin' choppy,
Thar's a yank on his line like his rope caught a croppy.

Thar's a clang o' fish-buckets; on the waves thar's a war;
An' his arms from their sockets they nearly is tore.

All the Portygees squallin', an' the trouble is now,
An' thar's no horn to hitch to; but he bawls, "Hook 'em cow !"

Fer he'd roped a hoss-mackerel o' gorgeous degree,
An' she bucked double-barrelled, as she bruk from the sea.

Here that tuna come a-tunin'. Then his fish-line give a crack.
An' next thing, Billy Bowlegs was astride of her back.

He was spray-plowin' pronto, he was lost to the land,
For that hoss-fish was pullin' for the sea's Rio Grande.

She was rainbowin' fancy, fulla spite chockablock,
An' he larned about the fish tribe from soda to hock.

Whar they watched from the piers, whar they goggled from the bay,
All they saw goin' flyin' was a white sail o' spray.

But he never pulled leather, when she'd plunge or when she'd breach,
An' he rode her roun' the harbor an' bulldogged her on the beach. . . .

Still, as great as I am tryin' to considubble avail,
I ain't told about Billy an' his meet-up with the whale.

237

He was took on a v'yage, in bad need of a change,
Where the blue Injian Ocean is a wide-open range.

An' the skipper o' the clipper, he fancied a tune,
So he'd brought along with him his faverit bassoon.

It's a tube with a mouthpiece, an' it made yer flesh creep
When the capting would finger out "The Cradle o' the Deep."

An' thar rose in the tropics a roarin' big moon,
An' the fishes all glittered to hear that bassoon.

Billy'd sit up in the cross-trees, an' the skipper would play
Where the moon on the wavelets made 'em brighter than day.

So that puncher, he waited. An' one night, in his bunk,
He found that the skipper was a-layin' dead drunk.

It was darker on deck, when Bill snagged the bassoon.
There was only up in heaven jest a crust of a moon.

But the crew was all forrard. Bill crep' to the starn,
An' them keys with his fingers he started to larn.

Now there roamed on that sea-range a right whale gone sad,
Since the big white beluga was all the new fad —

Though a white whale's a dolphin ! What you git from it are
Isinglass from its bladder — from its roe, caviare —

An' the right whale's a right whale. Yet still, times was bad.
So it moped aroun' the ocean, all alone, feelin' sad.

An' the one thing that griped it till the teardrop would fall
Was it wished it was musical, which it wasn't at all.

238

If you wish to be musical, and are not at all,
You write ballats like this here one, an' the tear-drop will fall.

Well, that night, in its tantrum, like a quiver on the swell,
That big whale heerd music, an' he says, "All is well !"

An' he swum then, an' he swum then — an' with some it is wimmen,
An' with some it is liquor — but with him it was hymnin'.

An' with him it was tunes you beat out with yer tail.
So it was that Billy Bowlegs met up with that whale.

For he'd got hot and goin'; an' he made that whale weep
With the groans an' the sobbin' of "The Cradle of the Deep."

Then the whale hove up a mountain. Could that lusty heart fail ?
But, you see, this here Billy, he had never *seed* a whale !

An' its little eye trickled salt tears on the sea.
Like a butte on Wind River it appeared for to be.

It was vast, and it quivered, and it sidled longside,
An' some sailor yelled, "Blow me !" An' pore Bill lost his pride.

Fer it nudged with its shoulder, at the ship, an' the motion
Made it skid full o' ripples through the Injian Ocean.

An' Bill thought, "We'll never be saved, by a miracle !" . . .
But the nose of the whale has a blowhole or spiracle,

An' that whale shot a spout full o' brine in the air
As it clumsily curtsied, bein' glad it was there.

So it rained upon Billy, in the midst of his tune —
An' he pitched at the whale's nose the skipper's bassoon.

239

I dunno how he struck it, but up to the shank
In the hole o' the spiracle o' the right whale it sank;

An' that whale give a start, an' he sounded fer fair.
The wave h'isted the clipper, 'bout a mile in the air.

Thar was turrible upheavin's, thar was awful commotion,
An' it seemed like an earthquake had hit the dark ocean.

When the sea ceased ter welter, an' the wind ceased ter wail,
An' the elemental wrath might no longer avail —
They heerd distant music whar swam the great whale !

At the first kind o' strangled, an' as though it was coughin';
Then rele hauntin' music they heered from the offin';

Fer whenever it breathed, all its soul in one sigh,
That big seabeast bubbled an' poured music on high,

With the same the result of the skipper's bassoon . . .
An' it sailed away to starboard, still playin' a tune.

An' it swims, an' it swims — an' with some it is wimmen,
With some it is liquor — but with fish it is swimmin' —

An' swimmin' to music an' the thresh of its tail
Was the heaven of its yearnin' to that frustrated whale.

But the skipper was adamant, his bassoon was gone;
So he landed Billy Bowlegs at a port in Ceylon.

Which I don't know what become of him; perhaps he's still in jail,
All because o' bein' a cowboy not fittin' fer sail,
But somewhere, out in ocean, rich music will trail
Forever an' forever from a sweet-swimmin' whale . . .
O forever from a happy an' a star-spoutin' whale !

VIII

SONNETS

CENTENARY

Gerard Manley Hopkins
Born July 28, 1844

Through all the fissures of your appalled devotion,
language jetting — surf of afflicted sense
frothing — rush of an ocean of eloquence,
and, as illimitable archetype of that ocean,
Very God, constricted in mind and emotion,
in rote and ritual, yet deviser of all
inscape; the ocean gathering to fall
whelming stark rock, gritting and grinding erosion,
seeping through arid thirsting — You and Yours,
to that sea salt, as alum, or as the smell
of walnutleaf to wide air — what Scotus knew
to be particular and integral —
But O the tenth wave of the deep no flesh endures,
on a hair hung, to plunge and thunder over you !

July 31, 1944

GOD'S FIRE

I thought, reading "The Washers of the Shroud"
In Lowell's verse, half fustian and half great
Prevision of our growing western state
Then shaken by passage of the roaring cloud
Of civil war: he saw the Sisters Three
Of more than legend in that wan water wring
"The fatal raiment" of tyrant and of king,
Under the shadow of Life's towering tree,
Yet never dreamed what power might be unlocked:
Raging inferno, consuming lava pit,
Fury of flame, with life's foundations split.
Whether it change the world, or God be mocked,
Time was, Time is ! How fatefully the sound
Time shall be ! tolls. Prometheus is unbound.

TWO SONNETS OF PAUL

I

Paul stood on Mars' hill in the highest court
Of Athens, and they thought, "His word is strange !"
Yet hearkened, who were ever seeking change,
With Areopagus their last resort.
Paul said, "I know where ye have darkly trod,
But come to make as diamond your seeing
Of Him in whom you live and have your being,
Who have raised your altar to The Unknown God.

Out of mere nothing, we; and in His breath
Only endure !" Then Dionysius heard
And Damaris, nor mocked the apostle's word
Speaking new knowledge both of life and death.
But most abode in safety with what was known:
The image of God in fondled gold or stone.

II

Paul to Galatia spake of Abraham's sons,
One born of bondmaid, one of a woman free;
Two simple covenants for all to see
Of flesh and spirit. The allegory runs
Of cities; but the bondage that was once
To flesh, of spirit, still is like to be.
Yet Paul declared, "We are called to liberty
Which is the spirit that our bondage shuns. . . .

245

We are the children of promise. We shall reap
Life everlasting !" Writing thus from Rome
Beyond Propontis the shining word went home,
Far over Patmos lit the Aegean deep,
Till, like an earthquake, the tremor of it was come
Even to Antioch and Iconium.

THE EXCLUSIVE CLUB

It was an exclusive club. With quiet feet
And deferent mien, smooth servants brought you things.
Men sat in overstuffed chairs like overstuffed kings.
Some slept. In some the heart had ceased to beat.
They were well protected from the cold and heat,
Were well connected, as were those they knew.
A few had really rowed upon the crew.
All enjoyed revenue and things to eat.

They were married to women of charm and cultivation.
They had lovely homes and grounds and knew good wine.
They wintered on currycombed beaches. They liked to dine
And collect expensive things, without ostentation.
The one who had bought me drinks coughed, bowed his head.
Almost in a whisper, "Oh dear God !" he said.

THE WEB

All men are flies now in the corporate web.
No longer in the open field of power
the rough and ready fighter finds his hour
where the great tides of trading flow and ebb.
No longer men are bullies in the land;
but huge amalgamations of resource
flourish in factions of opposing force.
And still the people, pillaged on every hand !

Our press, our legislators, even our state,
caught in such meshes by a thousand ties
of interest — can they, or we, grow wise
to mould for all mankind a nation great
above its Timons, gathering up the gage
of a miraculous and heroic age ?

A WALLED GARDEN

To Hogarth's dust, "great painter of mankind"

There Hogarth's bullfinch rests. *"Alas, poor Dick !"*
The carved stone read, against the garden wall,
When the great limner still was with the quick
And his old mulberry tree branched wide and tall
Where foundling children feasted on its fruit
When Chiswick was a place of field and lane
For "Nature's school," before the rising bruit
Of the industrial Cities of the Plain.

The bright-eyed satirist died in Leicester Square
Whose crayon caught "the business of the scene,"
But only briefly did he linger there,
Returning soon to haunts where he had been
One, with his bullfinch, of the country kind,
"Whose pictur'd Morals" (Garrick) "chain the mind."

GANYMEDE

Let us propitiate poetic ghosts
who mop and mow along those bogus lines
empty of any phrase to crinkle spines,
(to some few ancients sycophantic hosts)
who miss the liquor but gulp up the toasts,
flatter their little egos to the nines,
and cut their etymological monkeyshines
With flibbertigibbet flouncings and shrill boasts . . .

Let us appease these dead? Oh, let us not,
nor seek the dead — but leave them to dry rot!
But climb the cliff whence that great eagle flies
who saw from heaven fire trailing in a reed,
who fastened — shoulder and thigh — on Ganymede
and hoisted mortal beauty to the skies!

PLANTATION ON THE JAMES

The Fiend's own racket rouses all Poplar Hill
As horses and mules and cows dash up the lane.
The University bloods are at it again,
And Thomas and Miles are laughing fit to kill !
With tails that flourish a tin-pan codicil
The livestock clatter and flee their urgent bane
Young Edgar Allan, cloaked like a don of Spain,
Devilish handsome, herding with right good will. . . .

And then in the octagon room with the alcove niche,
And bust of Pallas, and high four-poster bed,
Where summer moonlight over the floor is shed
On dark bent head, while cavernous glooms enrich
The night — what haunted palace, what fountained shrine,
What murmur. "The viol, the violet, and the vine !"

BYRON AT OSTEND

"As soon as he reached his room Lord Byron fell like a thunderbolt upon the chambermaid."

DR. POLIDORI

Not the gier-eagle stooping from his gyre,
Not the tail-twitching leopard on a limb,
(Just possibly) were fitting peer for him
Who of all rhetoric seems the robust sire,
Adroit with keen rapier of satire,
And songful like the very cherubim,
As when the isles of Greece through sunset swim
Roused by a more than Apollonian lyre.

So why anticipate a Sterne's finesse
In conduct — and inn-conduct ? Quickly turn
To Jove and Danaë — classical allusion !
No ambiguity softens such address;
Vast was the madness that knew all ways to burn —
Profound is the professorial confusion !

THE PENANCE

They say that Joan of Arc met Gilles de Rais
On some phantasmal bridge that Heaven employs
For penance: she of heavenly voices fey,
He the unspeakable beast who murdered boys,
Black with the fires of hell.
                              His Saint (reviled
Long since by those who always must deface,
Defame, destroy) smiled on him like a child
Or like the martyr in Rouen marketplace. . . .

Ah then, at Ambiéres, he made them yield
Before his furious feats of arms; ah then,
Once more the Maid's protector in the field
He stormed . . . and did he hear her breathe again,
"Faithful and valorous !" . . . From the misted spheres
His groans were iron. Like blood-streams fell his tears.

FULVIA

Male beauty she knew, and knew the forum's rant
Tragically. Was Milo worth the sweat,
When Clodius fell ? Cleopatra was not yet.
Earlier corrupt, she deemed orations cant
Even on the dark and desperate Catiline,
Even by the greatest since Demosthenes,
Now Antony was god, his enemies
Demons. What house burned on the Palatine
When Pulcher set the torch ? "Nay, Cicero,"
To the severed head she cried, "Here's eloquence,
Invective — from this mouth the viper stung !"
Her own Philippi unprescient yet to know,
And all the endless woe proceeding thence,
She glittered, and drove her needle through his tongue.

HATE

I saw hate once in the eyes of an alligator
And once in the eyes of a man; the first begot
By nature; the second by I know not what.
I shuddered at the creature, the fated hater.
But the man, the man was tragic. Like a skull
He stared at me, dead white; he endured somewhere
A throe like death, for death was in his stare.
Scarce he drew breath. His eyes were blank and dull.

It is a seizure horrible to behold,
Pure hate; a thing of awe, like all things pure.
It is something flesh and blood can scarce endure,
Being somehow older than life. Can it be as old
As God, as evil and good ? I am only sure
That passion and anger are hot; but hate is cold.

IX

PENDANT

WHOSE?

Scientifical or empirical,
Whose intellection do you call
The fundamental miracle
That anything should exist at all?

THE FRUIT

It is good to drink whiskey,
to clasp a woman,
to sing in the morning,
to scan the sky,
to laugh and be frisky,
to love and be human —
but what if you die ?

Well, die you must,
die you will surely !
Sifted to dust
that phenomenal brain !
Your love and your lust,
The thought you thought purely,
will not remain.

Or will they remain —
if lovers and thinkers,
touched by the beauty
of sea or sky,
feel, as it were
like a nag in blinkers,
their life go by ?

Pierced then to the root
By confounding glory,
hear them cry, "Oh look !"
hear them shout, "Oh see !"
That'll be the fruit
of your ignorant story,
as it will with me.

OUTLIER

The old wolf lies with his nose on his paws
far off on a dreambound hill.
He blinks an eye over man-made laws
and snuffs the air for the kill. . . .

Running at night, running at night,
with the wind-in-the-wood's caress,
with the moon day-bright on the rock-torn height
like a queen in her wedding dress.

Not his with the pack to howl and gloat,
with the kept curs whine and bark;
there is salt on his tongue and fire in his throat
for his mate who runs in the dark. . . .

Running at night, running at night,
with the long swift lope of ease,
springy tendons, pads feather-light,
and her form that flits through the trees.

Burdocked his fell and his red eye dim
and his muzzle grizzled and grey,
but the stars of heaven crowd down on him
though a million miles away. . . .

Running at night, running at night,
with the first wild rush of youth,
with the moon in flight, with the stars in flight,
so close on the heels of truth.

The old wolf grunts his scorn of the pack,
though cold be close to the bone;
who climbed the track that would not turn back,
who halts on the rock alone. . . .

Running at night, running at night,
past mortal thought and breath:
beast with a God just beyond his sight
to track through the mist of death.

THE NIGHT IN THE FIELD

"It is night," said the Voice. "Thick darkness covers the Earth.
Yet kings shall come to the brightness of this rising.
Lift your eyes!" it said. "I say this thing shall be
Where snow under stars is white, where the stir of the Northern
  tree
Moans like your desolate sea.
Let your heart enlarge, and fear not for this birth,
Nor find this hour surprising!"

Then I dreamed that beneath the fir tree, under the pine,
Beneath snow-burdened spruce boughs brushing low,
Through all that diamond-dust of gusty snow,
Under a star as bright as a spear, or a tear,
Came strangely in long line
The camels out of Midian footing slow
And Sheba's dromedaries on desert ways,
Swaying across the pasture out of starbright haze,
Bringing the gold, the incense, and the praise. . . .

On the long slope, the mounded bushes moved
Like flocks of Kedar, gathered all together
With rams of Nebaioth, against the weather
Drifted and driven as the night wind roved.
Glamour was scattered of a ghostly story.
And the Voice said, "Lo, I bring my sons from far,
Their silver and gold upon them. Where they are
They come with acceptance into the house of my glory!"

And I saw, as though they bowed, the pine and fir
Draw back — the ancient glory of Lebanon!
The humble stable, as in days that were,

How simply with breathing cattle it glowed and shone
"Where violence and destruction are no more !"
Underneath fragrant branches. And the Voice
Echoing in my soul said, as my head was bowed,
"Despair not, Mortal ! O rejoice, rejoice !
As the doves to their windows, see who fly like cloud !
For a little one has become as a thousand strong,
A small one a great nation, on this night. . . .
I the Lord will hasten it in his time !"

Then it waned on the winter wind, like the sound of song.
Yet the light on the snow seemed an everlasting light.
And the wind changed. And I heard the bells in chime.

ACKNOWLEDGMENTS

My thanks for permission to reprint certain poems originally appearing in their pages to *The Saturday Review of Literature, Voices, The Atlantic Monthly, The University of Kansas City Review, The Holy Cross Purple, The New York Times, The New York Times Sunday Magazine, The New Yorker, Encore,* and *The Gloucester Times.*

THE TYPE

This book was set on the Linotype in Janson, a recutting made direct from the type cast from matrices (now in possession of the Stempel foundry, Frankfurt am Main) made by Anton Janson some time between 1660 and 1687.

Of Janson's origin nothing is known. He may have been a relative of Justus Janson, a printer of Danish birth who practised in Leipzig from 1614 to 1635. Some time between 1657 and 1668 Anton Janson, a punch-cutter and type-founder, bought from the Leipzig printer Johann Erich Hahn the type-foundry which had formerly been a part of the printing house of M. Friedrich Lankisch. Janson's types were first shown in a specimen sheet issued at Leipzig about 1675. Janson's successor, and perhaps his son-in-law, Johann Karl Edling, issued a specimen sheet of Janson types in 1689. His heirs sold the Janson matrices in Holland to Wolffgang Dietrich Erhardt.

The book was composed, printed, and bound by The Plimpton Press, Norwood, Massachusetts. Typography and binding based on original designs by W. A. Dwiggins.